THE ROYAL HORTICULTURAL SOCIETY
DIARY 2006

Commentary by Brent Elliott
Illustrations from
the Royal Horticultural Society's Lindley Library

TED SMART

Frances Lincoln Limited
4 Torriano Mews
Torriano Avenue
London NW5 2RZ
www.franceslincoln.com

The Royal Horticultural Society Diary 2006
Copyright © Frances Lincoln Limited 2005

An interest in gardening is all you need to enjoy being a member of the RHS.

Website: www.rhs.org.uk

British Library cataloguing-in-publication data
A catalogue record for this book is available from the British Library

ISBN 0-7112-2582-6

Printed in China

First Frances Lincoln edition 2004
This edition produced for The Book People Ltd, Hall Wood Avenue, Haydock, St Helens WA11 9UL

RHS FLOWER SHOWS 2006

All shows feature a wide range of floral exhibits staged by the nursery trade, with associated competitions reflecting seasonal changes and horticultural sundries. With the exception of the shows held at Cardiff, Malvern, Chelsea, Wisley, Hampton Court and Tatton Park, all RHS Flower Shows will be held in one or both of the Society's Horticultural Halls in Greycoat Street and Vincent Square, Westminster, London SW1.

The dates given are correct at the time of going to press, but before travelling to a show, we strongly advise you to check with the Diary Dates section of the RHS journal *The Garden*, or telephone the 24-hour Flower Show Information Line (020 7649 1885) for the latest details.

COVER
A hand-coloured engraving after a drawing by Miss S.A. Drake (*fl.* 1820s–1840s) of *Disa grandiflora*, from John Lindley's *Sertum orchidaceum* (1838–1841)

TITLE PAGE
A watercolour drawing (1828) of a 'Scarlet Flake' carnation, dating from the late eighteenth century, with some jasmine, *Jasminum officinale*

OVERLEAF
A watercolour drawing (1820) of *Viola tricolor*

CALENDAR 2006

JANUARY	FEBRUARY	MARCH	APRIL
M T W T F S S	M T W T F S S	M T W T F S S	M T W T F S S
1	1 2 3 4 5	1 2 3 4 5	1 2
2 3 4 5 6 7 8	6 7 8 9 10 11 12	6 7 8 9 10 11 12	3 4 5 6 7 8 9
9 10 11 12 13 14 15	13 14 15 16 17 18 19	13 14 15 16 17 18 19	10 11 12 13 14 15 16
16 17 18 19 20 21 22	20 21 22 23 24 25 26	20 21 22 23 24 25 26	17 18 19 20 21 22 23
23 24 25 26 27 28 29	27 28	27 28 29 30 31	24 25 26 27 28 29 30
30 31			

MAY	JUNE	JULY	AUGUST
M T W T F S S	M T W T F S S	M T W T F S S	M T W T F S S
1 2 3 4 5 6 7	1 2 3 4	1 2	1 2 3 4 5 6
8 9 10 11 12 13 14	5 6 7 8 9 10 11	3 4 5 6 7 8 9	7 8 9 10 11 12 13
15 16 17 18 19 20 21	12 13 14 15 16 17 18	10 11 12 13 14 15 16	14 15 16 17 18 19 20
22 23 24 25 26 27 28	19 20 21 22 23 24 25	17 18 19 20 21 22 23	21 22 23 24 25 26 27
29 30 31	26 27 28 29 30	24 25 26 27 28 29 30	28 29 30 31
		31	

SEPTEMBER	OCTOBER	NOVEMBER	DECEMBER
M T W T F S S	M T W T F S S	M T W T F S S	M T W T F S S
1 2 3	1	1 2 3 4 5	1 2 3
4 5 6 7 8 9 10	2 3 4 5 6 7 8	6 7 8 9 10 11 12	4 5 6 7 8 9 10
11 12 13 14 15 16 17	9 10 11 12 13 14 15	13 14 15 16 17 18 19	11 12 13 14 15 16 17
18 19 20 21 22 23 24	16 17 18 19 20 21 22	20 21 22 23 24 25 26	18 19 20 21 22 23 24
25 26 27 28 29 30	23 24 25 26 27 28 29	27 28 29 30	25 26 27 28 29 30 31
	30 31		

CALENDAR 2007

JANUARY	FEBRUARY	MARCH	APRIL
M T W T F S S	M T W T F S S	M T W T F S S	M T W T F S S
1 2 3 4 5 6 7	1 2 3 4	1 2 3 4	1
8 9 10 11 12 13 14	5 6 7 8 9 10 11	5 6 7 8 9 10 11	2 3 4 5 6 7 8
15 16 17 18 19 20 21	12 13 14 15 16 17 18	12 13 14 15 16 17 18	9 10 11 12 13 14 15
22 23 24 25 26 27 28	19 20 21 22 23 24 25	19 20 21 22 23 24 25	16 17 18 19 20 21 22
29 30 31	26 27 28	26 27 28 29 30 31	23 24 25 26 27 28 29
			30

MAY	JUNE	JULY	AUGUST
M T W T F S S	M T W T F S S	M T W T F S S	M T W T F S S
1 2 3 4 5 6	1 2 3	1	1 2 3 4 5
7 8 9 10 11 12 13	4 5 6 7 8 9 10	2 3 4 5 6 7 8	6 7 8 9 10 11 12
14 15 16 17 18 19 20	11 12 13 14 15 16 17	9 10 11 12 13 14 15	13 14 15 16 17 18 19
21 22 23 24 25 26 27	18 19 20 21 22 23 24	16 17 18 19 20 21 22	20 21 22 23 24 25 26
28 29 30 31	25 26 27 28 29 30	23 24 25 26 27 28 29	27 28 29 30 31
		30 31	

SEPTEMBER	OCTOBER	NOVEMBER	DECEMBER
M T W T F S S	M T W T F S S	M T W T F S S	M T W T F S S
1 2	1 2 3 4 5 6 7	1 2 3 4	1 2
3 4 5 6 7 8 9	8 9 10 11 12 13 14	5 6 7 8 9 10 11	3 4 5 6 7 8 9
10 11 12 13 14 15 16	15 16 17 18 19 20 21	12 13 14 15 16 17 18	10 11 12 13 14 15 16
17 18 19 20 21 22 23	22 23 24 25 26 27 28	19 20 21 22 23 24 25	17 18 19 20 21 22 23
24 25 26 27 28 29 30	29 30 31	26 27 28 29 30	24 25 26 27 28 29 30
			31

INTRODUCTION

During the eighteenth and nineteenth centuries, drawing was considered a suitable skill for a woman to acquire. Few women achieved fame as botanical artists within their lifetimes, but a handful of names show that it was possible: for example, Mary Lawrance, who published books of rose and passionflower portraits at the end of the eighteenth century; and Priscilla Bury, whose *Hexandrian Plants* (1831–4) is a masterpiece of the genre. Far more drew flowers as a hobby. Of those discovered and published in recent times, the best known is Edith Holden, whose nature notes for 1906 were published as *The Country Diary of an Edwardian Lady* in 1977; more recently, Richard Mabey's *Flowers of May* and Todd Gray's *Victorian Wild Flowers of Devon* have brought unknown artists to light. The work of many more no doubt lurks in family papers, boxes or attics, or even library cupboards.

Some time in the late nineteenth or early twentieth century – the exact year is unknown – William Wilks, the Secretary of the Royal Horticultural Society, was offered three volumes of drawings by three different vendors. The drawings were all by the same artist and were in chronological order, the first volume ran from 1808 to 1825, the second from 1832 to 1842, the third from 1842 to 1852. Wilks paid £6 and £8 respectively for the second two volumes; it is not known what he paid for the first. And so more than 300 drawings by Caroline Maria Applebee entered the Society's collection.

Biographical research has yielded little information. Caroline Maria Applebee was born in London in the late eighteenth century, and died in London in 1854. It seems likely that she was upper middle class, because of the number of greenhouse and conservatory plants she drew: it was not until the middle of the nineteenth century, after taxes on glass, bricks and wood were abolished, that ownership of a greenhouse became widespread. She seems to have lived, or at least spent time, in Essex: one of the binders of the volumes was a Colchester firm.

Applebee's earliest drawings must have been made while she was still virtually a child. Her handling of details such as leaf venation improved as she became more experienced, but her skills at composition were apparent from the beginning. The horticultural fashions of the day can be traced in her work: her first volume contains drawings of tulips, and the second ranunculus; in the final volume the florist's calceolaria appears. She also drew wild flowers from the fields and hedgerows. This work, and that of other female painters who documented their local flora, may help current studies of local biodiversity by providing a standard for comparison with the flora of the present.

The three volumes do not cover the years 1825–32. Was there originally another volume? If so, where is it today? Perhaps it is hiding in *your* family papers.

Brent Elliott
The Royal Horticultural Society

December & January

26 Monday

Boxing Day (St Stephen's Day)
Holiday, UK, Republic of Ireland, Canada, USA, Australia and
New Zealand (Christmas Day observed)

27 Tuesday

Holiday, UK, Republic of Ireland, Canada,
Australia and New Zealand (Boxing Day observed)

28 Wednesday

29 Thursday

30 Friday

31 Saturday

New Moon
New Year's Eve

1 Sunday

New Year's Day

A watercolour drawing (1846) of the holm oak, *Quercus ilex*, and the Kermes oak, *Quercus coccifera*

January

Monday **2**

Holiday, UK, Republic of Ireland, Canada,
USA, Australia and New Zealand

Tuesday **3**

Holiday, Scotland and New Zealand

Wednesday **4**

Thursday **5**

Friday **6**

First Quarter
Epiphany

Saturday **7**

Sunday **8**

A watercolour drawing (1835) of *Hippeastrum vittatum*, a South American bulbous plant

January

9 Monday

---

10 Tuesday

---

11 Wednesday

---

12 Thursday

---

13 Friday

---

14 Saturday

Full Moon

15 Sunday

A watercolour drawing (1841) of the Christmas rose, *Helleborus niger*

January

Monday **16**

Holiday, USA (Martin Luther King's birthday)

Tuesday **17**

RHS London Flower Show

Wednesday **18**

RHS London Flower Show

Thursday **19**

Friday **20**

Saturday **21**

Sunday **22**

Last Quarter

A watercolour drawing (1820) of a group of *Daphne cneorum, Jasminum nudiflorum, Omphalodes verna* and *Dicentra eximia*

January

23 Monday

24 Tuesday

25 Wednesday

26 Thursday

Holiday, Australia (Australia Day)

27 Friday

28 Saturday

29 Sunday

New Moon
Chinese New Year

A watercolour drawing (1835) of *Crocus aureus* and *Crocus pulchellus*

January & February

Monday **30**

Tuesday **31**

Islamic New Year (subject to sighting of the moon)

Wednesday **1**

Thursday **2**

Friday **3**

Saturday **4**

Sunday **5**

First Quarter

A watercolour drawing (1847) of *Camellia 'Donckelaeri'*

WEEK 6

February

6 Monday

Holiday, New Zealand (Waitangi Day)

7 Tuesday

8 Wednesday

9 Thursday

10 Friday

11 Saturday

12 Sunday

Lincoln's birthday

A watercolour drawing (1830) of *Anemone pavonina* and *Gentiana acaulis*

February

Monday **13**

Full Moon
Holiday (observed), USA

Tuesday **14**

St Valentine's Day
RHS London Flower Show

Wednesday **15**

RHS London Flower Show

Thursday **16**

Friday **17**

Saturday **18**

Sunday **19**

A watercolour drawing (1843) of *Ranunculus asiaticus* and *Dianthus caryophyllus*

February

20 Monday

Holiday, USA (Presidents' Day)

21 Tuesday

Last Quarter

22 Wednesday

23 Thursday

24 Friday

25 Saturday

26 Sunday

A watercolour drawing (1837) of the snake's-head fritillary, *Fritillaria meleagris*

February & March

Monday **27**

Tuesday **28**

New Moon
Shrove Tuesday

Wednesday **1**

Ash Wednesday
St David's Day

Thursday **2**

Friday **3**

Saturday **4**

Sunday **5**

A watercolour drawing (1835) of an unnamed auricula cultivar

March

6 Monday

First Quarter

7 Tuesday

8 Wednesday

9 Thursday

10 Friday

11 Saturday

12 Sunday

A watercolour drawing (1835) of a group of *Alstroemeria pelegrina, Nemophila menziesii* and *Oxalis versicolor*

March

Monday **13**

Commonwealth Day

Tuesday **14**

Full Moon
RHS London Flower Show

Wednesday **15**

RHS London Flower Show

Thursday **16**

Friday **17**

St Patrick's Day
Holiday, Northern Ireland and Republic of Ireland

Saturday **18**

Orchid Show

Sunday **19**

RHS Orchid Show

A watercolour drawing (1822) of a wallflower, *Erysimum* (formerly *Cheiranthus*) *cheiri*, and a stock, *Matthiola incana*

March

20 Monday

Vernal Equinox

21 Tuesday

22 Wednesday

Last Quarter

23 Thursday

24 Friday

25 Saturday

26 Sunday

Mothering Sunday, UK
British Summertime begins

A watercolour drawing (1815) of three tulips, 'The Claude', 'Duke of Sutherland' and 'Duchess of Montrose'

March & April

Monday **27**

Tuesday **28**

Wednesday **29**

New Moon

Thursday **30**

Friday **31**

Saturday **1**

Moderate pruning can now begin

Sunday **2**

A watercolour drawing (1847) of a group of *Nemophila menziesii, Ceanothus azureus*
and *Nemophila atro-purpurea*, North American plants introduced in the early nineteenth century

April

3 Monday

4 Tuesday

5 Wednesday

First Quarter

6 Thursday

7 Friday

8 Saturday

9 Sunday

Palm Sunday

A watercolour drawing (1824) of two tulips, 'The Claude' and 'Duke of Sutherland'

April

Monday **10**

Tuesday **11**

RHS London Flower Show

Wednesday **12**

RHS London Flower Show

Thursday **13**

Full Moon
Maundy Thursday
Passover (Pesach), First Day

Friday **14**

Good Friday
Holiday, UK, Republic of Ireland,
Canada, USA, Australia and New Zealand

Saturday **15**

Sunday **16**

Easter Sunday

A watercolour drawing (1841) of the lily-of-the-valley, *Convallaria majalis*

April

---

17 Monday

Easter Monday
Holiday, UK (exc. Scotland), Republic of Ireland,
Canada, Australia and New Zealand

---

18 Tuesday

---

19 Wednesday

Passover (Pesach), Seventh Day

---

20 Thursday

Passover (Pesach), Eighth Day

---

21 Friday

Last Quarter
Birthday of Queen Elizabeth II

---

22 Saturday

---

23 Sunday

St George's Day

A watercolour drawing (1843) of a Japanese iris

April

Monday **24**

Apply spring feed for Roses

Tuesday **25**

Holiday, Australia and New Zealand (Anzac Day)

Wednesday **26**

Thursday **27**

New Moon

Friday **28**

Saturday **29**

Sunday **30**

A watercolour drawing (1820) of *Ranunculus asiaticus* and *Papaver orientale*

May

1 Monday

Make a May Hanging Basket ~~p147 Alan T~~

p147 Alan T

Early May Bank Holiday, UK and Republic of Ireland

2 Tuesday

3 Wednesday

4 Thursday

5 Friday

First Quarter

6 Saturday

Add layer of compost as a mulch

7 Sunday

A watercolour drawing (1843) of a Japanese iris

May

Monday **8**

Tuesday **9**

Wednesday **10**

Thursday **11**

Malvern Spring Gardening Show (to be confirmed)

Friday **12**

Malvern Spring Gardening Show

Saturday **13**

Full Moon
Malvern Spring Gardening Show

Sunday **14**

Mother's Day, Canada, USA, Australia and New Zealand
Malvern Spring Gardening Show

A watercolour drawing (1831) of a moss rose, *Rosa* x *centifolia* 'Muscosa'

May

15 Monday

16 Tuesday

17 Wednesday

18 Thursday

19 Friday

20 Saturday

Last Quarter

21 Sunday

A watercolour drawing (1834) of forms of *Dianthus chinensis*, the Chinese or Indian pink

May

Monday **22**

Tuesday **23**

Chelsea Flower Show

Wednesday **24**

Chelsea Flower Show

Thursday **25**

Ascension Day
Chelsea Flower Show

Friday **26**

Chelsea Flower Show

Saturday **27**

New Moon
Chelsea Flower Show (to be confirmed)

Sunday **28**

A watercolour drawing (1834) of *Magnolia hypoleuca*

May & June

29 Monday

Spring Bank Holiday, UK
Holiday, USA (Memorial Day)

30 Tuesday

31 Wednesday

1 Thursday

2 Friday

Jewish Feast of Weeks (Shavuot)

3 Saturday

First Quarter

4 Sunday

Whit Sunday (Pentecost)

A watercolour drawing (1833) of the heartsease or wild pansy, *Viola tricolor*

June

Monday **5**

Holiday, Republic of Ireland
Holiday, New Zealand (The Queen's birthday)

Tuesday **6**

Wednesday **7**

Thursday **8**

Friday **9**

Saturday **10**

The Queen's official birthday (subject to confirmation)

Sunday **11**

Full Moon
Trinity Sunday

A watercolour drawing (1848) of myrtle, *Myrtus communis*, and a hybrid verbena

June

12 Monday

Holiday, Australia (The Queen's birthday)

13 Tuesday

14 Wednesday

BBC Gardeners' World Live, Birmingham

15 Thursday

Corpus Christi
BBC Gardeners' World Live, Birmingham

16 Friday

BBC Gardeners' World Live, Birmingham

17 Saturday

BBC Gardeners' World Live, Birmingham

18 Sunday

Last Quarter
Father's Day, UK, Canada and USA
BBC Gardeners' World Live, Birmingham

A watercolour drawing (1832) of *Senecio elegans* and *Trollius europaeus*

June

Monday **19**

Tuesday **20**

Wednesday **21**

Summer Solstice

Thursday **22**

Friday **23**

Saturday **24**

Sunday **25**

New Moon

A watercolour drawing (1847) of early petunia hybrids, *Petunia integrifolia* x *nyctaginiflora*

June & July

26 Monday

27 Tuesday

28 Wednesday

29 Thursday

30 Friday

1 Saturday

Holiday, Canada (Canada Day)

2 Sunday

A watercolour drawing (1848) of *Iris pseudacorus* and *Carex pendula*

July

Monday **3**

First Quarter

Tuesday **4**

Holiday, USA (Independence Day)

Wednesday **5**

Thursday **6**

Friday **7**

Saturday **8**

Sunday **9**

A watercolour drawing (1839) of *Convolvulus tricolor*,
a Mediterranean bindweed cultivated since the seventeenth century

July

10 Monday

11 Tuesday

Full Moon
Hampton Court Palace Flower Show

12 Wednesday

Holiday, Northern Ireland (Battle of the Boyne)
Hampton Court Palace Flower Show

13 Thursday

Hampton Court Palace Flower Show

14 Friday

Hampton Court Palace Flower Show

15 Saturday

St Swithin's Day
Hampton Court Palace Flower Show

16 Sunday

Hampton Court Palace Flower Show

A watercolour drawing (1830) of sweet peas, *Lathyrus odoratus*

July

Monday **17**

Last Quarter

Tuesday **18**

Wednesday **19**

Thursday **20**

Friday **21**

Saturday **22**

Sunday **23**

A watercolour drawing (1826) of fruits (raspberries, gooseberries, red and white currants)

July

24 Monday

25 Tuesday

New Moon

26 Wednesday

The RHS Flower Show at Tatton Park

27 Thursday

The RHS Flower Show at Tatton Park

28 Friday

The RHS Flower Show at Tatton Park

29 Saturday

The RHS Flower Show at Tatton Park

30 Sunday

The RHS Flower Show at Tatton Park

A watercolour drawing (1849) of *Fuchsia denticulata*
(known to Caroline Maria Applebee as *Fuchsia serratifolia*)

July & August

Monday **31**

Tuesday **1**

Wednesday **2**

First Quarter

Thursday **3**

Friday **4**

Saturday **5**

Sunday **6**

A watercolour drawing (1834) of *Hibiscus trionum*, known in Applebee's time as the bladder ketmia

August

7 Monday

Summer Bank Holiday, Scotland and Republic of Ireland

8 Tuesday

9 Wednesday

Full Moon

10 Thursday

11 Friday

12 Saturday

13 Sunday

A watercolour drawing (1832) of the small bindweed, *Convolvulus arvensis*

August

Monday **14**

Tuesday **15**

Wednesday **16**

Last Quarter

Thursday **17**

Friday **18**

Saturday **19**

Sunday **20**

A watercolour drawing (1820) of *Delphinium elatum*

August

21 Monday

22 Tuesday

Wisley August Flower Show

23 Wednesday

New Moon
Wisley August Flower Show

24 Thursday

Wisley August Flower Show

25 Friday

26 Saturday

27 Sunday

A watercolour drawing (1824) of a hollyhock, *Alcea rosea*

August & September

Monday **28**

Summer Bank Holiday, UK (exc. Scotland)

Tuesday **29**

Wednesday **30**

Thursday **31**

First Quarter

Friday **1**

Saturday **2**

Sunday **3**

Father's Day, Australia and New Zealand

A watercolour drawing (1824) of a French marigold, *Tagetes patula*

September

4 Monday

Holiday, Canada (Labour Day) and USA (Labor Day)

5 Tuesday

6 Wednesday

7 Thursday

Full Moon

8 Friday

9 Saturday

10 Sunday

A watercolour drawing (1835) of *Malope trifida*, a Mediterranean herb introduced in 1808

September

WEEK 37

Monday **11**

Tuesday **12**

RHS Late Summer Show, London

Wednesday **13**

RHS Late Summer Show, London

Thursday **14**

Last Quarter

Friday **15**

Saturday **16**

Sunday **17**

A watercolour drawing (1838) of *Gaillardia pulchella*, an American annual

September

---

18 Monday

---

19 Tuesday

---

20 Wednesday

---

21 Thursday

---

22 Friday

New Moon

---

23 Saturday

Autumnal Equinox
Jewish New Year (Rosh Hashanah)
Malvern Autumn Show

---

24 Sunday

First Day of Ramadân (subject to sighting of the moon)
Malvern Autumn Show

A watercolour drawing (1810) of *Callistephus chinensis* and *Coreopsis tinctoria*

September & October

Monday **25**

Tuesday **26**

Wednesday **27**

Thursday **28**

Friday **29**

Michaelmas Day

Saturday **30**

First Quarter

Sunday **1**

A watercolour drawing (1828) of a daylily, *Hemerocallis fulva*

October

2 Monday

Jewish Day of Atonement (Yom Kippur)
RHS Great Autumn Show (preview)

3 Tuesday

RHS Great Autumn Show

4 Wednesday

RHS Great Autumn Show

5 Thursday

6 Friday

7 Saturday

Full Moon
Jewish Festival of Tabernacles (Succoth), First Day

8 Sunday

A watercolour drawing (1847) of *Hebe speciosa*,
introduced from New Zealand a decade before the drawing was made

October

Monday **9**

Holiday, Canada (Thanksgiving Day)
Holiday, USA (Columbus Day)

Tuesday **10**

Wednesday **11**

Thursday **12**

Friday **13**

Saturday **14**

Last Quarter
Jewish Festival of Tabernacles (Succoth), Eighth Day

Sunday **15**

A watercolour drawing (1816) of the Californian poppy,
Eschscholzia californica, originally introduced in the 1790s as a species of *Chelidonium*

October

16 Monday

17 Tuesday

18 Wednesday

19 Thursday

20 Friday

21 Saturday

22 Sunday

New Moon

A watercolour drawing (1833) of *Salpiglossis* varieties

October

Monday **23**

Holiday, New Zealand (Labour Day)

Tuesday **24**

United Nations Day

Wednesday **25**

Thursday **26**

Friday **27**

Saturday **28**

Sunday **29**

First Quarter
British Summertime ends

A watercolour drawing (1833) of *Gladiolus psittacinus*
(now *Gladiolus dalenii*), introduced from South Africa in the mid-eighteenth century

October & November

30 Monday

Holiday, Republic of Ireland

31 Tuesday

Hallowe'en

1 Wednesday

All Saints' Day

2 Thursday

3 Friday

4 Saturday

5 Sunday

Full Moon
Guy Fawkes' Day

A watercolour drawing (1809) of *Dahlia pinnata*, one of the first dahlia introductions

November

Monday **6**

Tuesday **7**

Wednesday **8**

Thursday **9**

Friday **10**

RHS London Flower Show

Saturday **11**

Holiday, Canada (Remembrance Day) and USA (Veterans' Day)
RHS London Flower Show

Sunday **12**

Last Quarter
Remembrance Sunday, UK

A watercolour drawing (1847) of a wild bramble, *Rubus fruticosus*

November

13 Monday

14 Tuesday

15 Wednesday

16 Thursday

17 Friday

18 Saturday

19 Sunday

A watercolour drawing (1815) of filberts, *Corylus avellana*

November

Monday **20**

New Moon

Tuesday **21**

Wednesday **22**

Thursday **23**

Holiday, USA (Thanksgiving Day)

Friday **24**

Saturday **25**

Sunday **26**

A watercolour drawing (1850) of *Mahonia aquifolium,* an American shrub introduced in 1823

November & December

27 Monday

28 Tuesday

First Quarter

29 Wednesday

30 Thursday

St Andrew's Day

1 Friday

2 Saturday

3 Sunday

Advent Sunday

A watercolour drawing (1810) of the Chinese lantern, *Physalis alkekengi*

December

Monday **4**

Tuesday **5**

Full Moon

Wednesday **6**

Thursday **7**

Friday **8**

Saturday **9**

Sunday **10**

A watercolour drawing (1846) of an unnamed chrysanthemum variety

December

11 Monday

12 Tuesday

Last Quarter

13 Wednesday

14 Thursday

15 Friday

16 Saturday

Jewish Festival of Chanukah, First Day

17 Sunday

A watercolour drawing (1846) of mistletoe, cypress and cotoneaster

December

Monday **18**

Tuesday **19**

Wednesday **20**

New Moon

Thursday **21**

Friday **22**

Winter Solstice

Saturday **23**

Sunday **24**

Christmas Eve

A watercolour drawing (1833) of varieties of common holly, *Ilex aquifolium*

December

---

25 Monday

Christmas Day
Holiday, UK, Republic of Ireland,
Canada, USA, Australia and New Zealand

---

26 Tuesday

Boxing Day (St Stephen's Day)
Holiday, UK, Republic of Ireland, Canada, Australia and New Zealand

---

27 Wednesday

First Quarter

---

28 Thursday

---

29 Friday

---

30 Saturday

---

31 Sunday

New Year's Eve

A watercolour drawing (1845) of the guelder rose, *Viburnum opulus*

EUROPEAN NATIONAL HOLIDAYS 2006

AUSTRIA Jan. 1, 6; April 16, 17; May 1, 25; June 4, 5, 15; Aug. 15; Oct. 26; Nov. 1; Dec. 8, 25, 26

BELGIUM Jan. 1; April 16, 17; May 1, 25; June 4, 5; July 21; Aug. 15; Nov. 1, 11, 15; Dec. 25, 26

CYPRUS Jan. 1, 6; March 6, 25; April 1, 21, 23, 24; May 1; June 11, 12; Aug. 15; Oct. 1, 28; Dec. 25, 26

CZECH REPUBLIC Jan. 1; April 16, 17; May 1, 8; July 5, 6; Sept. 28; Oct. 28; Nov. 17; Dec. 24, 25, 26

DENMARK Jan. 1; April 13, 14, 16, 17; May 12, 25; June 4, 5; Dec. 25, 26

ESTONIA Jan. 1; Feb. 24; April 14, 16; May 1; June 4, 23, 24; Aug. 20; Dec. 25, 26

FINLAND Jan. 1, 6; April 14, 16, 17; May 1, 25; June 4, 24; Nov. 4; Dec. 6, 25, 26

FRANCE Jan. 1; April 16, 17; May 1, 8, 25; June 4, 5; July 14; Aug. 15; Nov. 1, 11; Dec. 25

GERMANY Jan. 1; April 14, 16, 17; May 1, 25; June 4, 5; Aug. 15; Oct. 3; Dec. 25, 26

GREECE Jan. 1, 6; March 6, 25; April 21, 23, 24; May 1; June 11, 12; Aug. 15; Oct. 28; Dec. 25, 26

HUNGARY Jan. 1; March 15; April 16, 17; May 1; June 4, 5; Aug. 20; Oct. 23; Nov. 1; Dec. 25, 26

ITALY Jan. 1, 6; April 16, 17, 25; May 1; June 2; Aug. 15; Nov. 1; Dec. 8, 25, 26

LATVIA Jan. 1; April 14, 16, 17; May 1; June 23, 24; Nov. 1, 18; Dec. 25, 26

LITHUANIA Jan 1; Feb. 16; March 11; April 16, 17; May 1; June 24; July 6; Aug. 15; Nov. 1; Dec. 25, 26

LUXEMBOURG Jan. 1; Feb. 27; April 14, 16; May 1, 25; June 4, 5, 23; Aug. 15; Nov. 1; Dec. 25, 26

MALTA Jan 1; Feb. 10; March 19, 31; April 14, 16; May 1; June 7, 29; Aug. 15; Sep. 8, 21; Dec. 8, 13, 25

NETHERLANDS Jan 1; April 14, 16, 17, 30; May 5, 25; June 4, 5; Dec. 25, 26

NORWAY Jan 1; April 13, 14, 16, 17; May 1, 17, 25; June 4, 5; Dec. 25, 26

POLAND Jan. 1; April 16, 17; May 1, 3; June 15; Aug. 15; Nov. 1, 11; Dec. 25, 26

PORTUGAL Jan. 1; Feb. 28; April 14, 16, 17, 25; May 1; June 10, 15; Aug. 15; Oct. 5; Nov. 1; Dec. 1, 8, 25

SLOVAKIA Jan. 1, 6; April 14, 16, 17; May 1, 8; July 5; Aug. 29; Sept. 1, 15; Nov. 1, 17; Dec. 24, 25, 26

SLOVENIA Jan. 1, 2; Feb. 8; April 16, 17, 27; May 1, 2; June 4; 25; Aug. 15; Oct. 31; Nov. 1; Dec. 25, 26

SPAIN Jan. 1, 6; March 19; April 14; 16; May 1; June 4; Aug. 15; Oct. 12; Nov. 1; Dec. 6, 8, 25

SWEDEN Jan. 1, 6; April 14, 16, 17; May 1, 25; June 4, 6, 24; Nov. 4, Dec. 25, 26

SWITZERLAND Jan. 1; April 14, 16, 17; May 1, 25; June 4, 5; Aug. 1; Dec. 25, 26

Decorating Plan of Action

① Move our bed & wardrobe.

② Get unit and find place in our room for my teaching
& Ian's papers.

③ Order new mattrass

④ Remove computer down stairs

⑤ Good clean of room.

⑥ Paint 3 walls

⑦ One wall paper

⑧ Get under bed storage.

⑨ Wardrobe + desk

⑩ Clear bookcase to just Matty's books

Matthew needs.
Wardrobe = £59.99   p786 · £90
desk - £29.99   p787.
under bed storage · p785 £11.99 /- 3
                        for videos etc.

Bed.   radiator

top
bar

Door

Adam needs
desk - from old pc table.   Bed ?

bookcase
Hifi trolly
new light
new curtains
flooring

our room for just now

1. Move bed / wardrobe to opposite sides
2. Move bookcase
3. add blank of drawers / files ?

THE GOLDEN YEARS

1954

text: David Sandison

design: Paul Kurzeja

SIENA

The world changed dramatically in 1954, often in ways which only the passing of time would reveal in full, but 20/20 hindsight lets us see clearly now. Politics, as ever, loomed large in events. In the United States, the increased arrogance of Senator Joseph McCarthy led him to believe he could take his anti-communist crusade to the heart of the establishment, and to his fall from power when the establishment bit back. Also in Washington, the US Supreme Court pronounced the end of a racially-divided educational system, but fired the starting gun on a decade of conflict.

In Vietnam, the Viet Minh's victory over occupying French forces created a two-nation Vietnam which would come to haunt the world in future years. In Egypt, the arrival of President Gamal Nasser would begin decades of confrontation as he set about building a modern state capable of leading the emerging oil-rich Arab nations.

From the terrible disasters which decimated BOAC's fleet of Comet jet airliners came knowledge and research which ensured that commercial air travel could develop and grow. A glimpse of the fascinating future came with

IBM's launch of the first commercially viable computer, while American and British scientists issued clear proof and warnings of the risks run by cigarette smokers everywhere.

A young medical student made history when he finally succeeded in breaking the 4-minute mile barrier, and Marilyn Monroe made headlines when she married an American legend, but divorced him almost before her signature dried on the wedding papers. In New York and Memphis, two singers recorded songs which would alter their - and our - lives forever.

The times, they were a'changing!

BOAC Ground Comets After Second Crash

ALL SEVEN COMET JET AIRLINERS, pride of the British Overseas Airways Corporation fleet, were grounded today following a mystery crash off the Mediterranean island of Elba with the loss of 35 lives.

It is the second disaster to hit the airline in the past 12 months. In May 1953 all 43 passengers and crew aboard another BOAC Comet were killed in a crash in India.

While BOAC chiefs ordered the immediate unladen return to London of all Comets so experts can carry out extensive tests on the world's first jet passenger plane, British and Italian investigators arrived in Elba to question 20 fishermen who witnessed the tragedy. Their evidence, that the Comet simply burst into flames and crashed into the sea, only reinforces theories that the British-built airliner has some form of inbuilt structural weakness which makes it prone to break-up when it meets air turbulence. Similar descriptions were given by witnesses to the Indian crash, which happened during a storm near Calcutta.

Pope Warns Of TV Danger

World moral guardians dismayed by the continuing impact and increased influence of television, received unconditional support from an important and infallible new ally today.

In Rome, Pope Pius XII spoke out strongly against the medium. Television was, he proclaimed, a potential threat to family life.

Queen Opens New Zealand Parliament

Queen Elizabeth II became the first reigning monarch to open a session of the New Zealand parliament in Wellington today, so keeping a promise she made in February 1952 when the death of her father King George VI forced her to abandon plans to visit Australia and New Zealand and return to London from a Kenyan safari holiday.

Death of Greenstreet, Ultimate Hollywood Heavy

A 'heavy' in every sense of the word, Sydney Greenstreet died today. Aged 75, the British-born actor was a remarkably late arrival to film stardom - he was 61 years old when he made his memorable screen debut as one of those hunting *The Maltese Falcon*. A great foil on that occasion for the laconic Humphrey Bogart, Greenstreet would loom large against Bogart again in *Casablanca* in 1942, going on to feature prominently in more than 20 other movies - most notably *Three Strangers*, *The Hucksters* and *The Woman In White*.

DiMaggio Weds Marilyn

A fairy-tale wedding in San Francisco today as baseball superstar Joe DiMaggio, one of America's greatest sporting heroes, married Hollywood star Marilyn Monroe.

It was to prove a Grimms-style fairy-tale. It was DiMaggio's second marriage, and led to his excommunication from a Roman Catholic church which did not recognize divorce. The couple argued incessantly and DiMaggio was incensed by Monroe's risqué sex scenes in *The Seven Year Itch*, especially the legendary 'skirt' scene.

Amid rumours of violence and complete incompatibility, the marriage of 'Joltin' Joe' and Marilyn would last a mere nine months.

ARRIVALS

Born this month:
21: Phil Thompson, Liverpool and England football player
29: Oprah Winfrey, Queen of American daytime TV

DEPARTURES

Died this month
11: Oscar Strauss, Austrian composer; Viscount John Simon, British statesman
18: Sydney Greenstreet, film actor *(see main story)*

NEWS IN BRIEF

8: President Eisenhower proposed to lower the US voting age from 21 to 18

12: In Rangoon, the Burmese government agreed the creation of Burmah Oil with three Western oil companies

15: In Kenya, the Mau Mau's military leader 'General China' was wounded and captured by British troops

21: The US Navy launched *Nautilus,* the world's first nuclear-powered submarine *(see picture)*

23: A total of 23 reported killed in accidents on frozen ice as severe weather hit Britain

JANUARY 25

BBC Airs 'Milk Wood'

Only two months after the sudden death of its author, the Welsh poet Dylan Thomas, in New York after a drinking session, the BBC today broadcast Under Milk Wood, the 'play for voices' the 39 year-old Thomas had spent almost 10 years writing and reworking.

Produced by Douglas Cleverdon and featuring an all-Welsh cast led by Richard Burton, the atmospheric, often ribald tale of life in a small fishing village was hailed as a masterpiece by critics and re-broadcast two days later to meet public demand.

Burton would also act as narrator on February 28 when Under Milk Wood had its first reading on the stage of London's Old Vic Theatre.

Nautilus: The world's first nuclear-powered submarine

JANUARY 1

US-Style Indicators For UK Cars

British motor manufacturers began revising the design of future models today as the government agreed to permit the introduction of flashing indicator lights.

Long a standard on American cars and subject of a strong lobbying campaign by Britain's motoring organizations and car-makers, the new lights will eventually replace old-fashioned 'flipper' indicators.

Built into the side window struts of cars, they were so ineffectual drivers were also obliged to give hand signals to ensure others were aware of imminent direction changes.

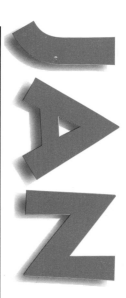

United Germany Plan Splits Super-Powers

FOREIGN MINISTERS OF THE United States, Britain, France and Soviet Russia clashed in Berlin today when they met to discuss plans to re-unite East and West Germany, divided since the end of World War II.

The sticking point was British minister Anthony Eden's proposal that an electoral law be drawn up to guarantee free elections in both halves of the country. This would lead initially to the creation of an all-German Assembly and ultimately an all-German government.

Russia's Vyacheslav Molotov rejected this outright, countering with a demand for the formation of an all-German government before elections. France, Britain and the US united in blocking this plan, which would legitimize an unelected East German puppet regime which is still unrecognized by the West.

Their argument is supported by figures released in West Berlin on January 1 which showed that more than 300,000 East Germans - almost 2 per cent of the population - had braved armed border patrols to reach the West in 1953.

Tito Fires His V-P

Yugoslavian President Josip Tito, apparently dedicated to creating one of the most enlightened communist regimes since his election in January 1953, today made it clear that he was not prepared to witness a move to democracy. Tito, a brilliant partisan leader whose guerrilla forces pinned down 12 German divisions during World War II, fired Vice-President Milovan Djilas - the man most widely assumed likely to succeed him - from the Communist Party's Central Committee. On January 26 his position was reinforced when he was re-elected Yugoslavia's leader.

Witch-Hunter McCarthy Angers Ike

SENATOR JOE McCARTHY - for the past five years one of America's most powerful and feared politicians as chairman of the House Un-American Activities Committee investigating alleged communist infiltration and influence in America - appears to have over-reached himself and brought himself into conflict with the White House.

Having created chaos in the film and television industries with damaging and often unsubstantiated charges against leading producers, directors and writers who then found themselves blacklisted, the Wisconsin senator began 1954 turning his spotlight on the US Army. Trouble began when McCarthy, carrying out a typical hectoring solo interrogation of a much-decorated Brigadier-General, told him he was 'a disgrace to his uniform' while pressing for information on an Army dentist accused of being a communist.

Enraged, Army Secretary Robert Stevens told McCarthy he would not allow officers to be treated that way. On February 23 the two met to attempt a settlement, but McCarthy released a statement which US newspapers read and reported as a climb-down by Stevens. Angered and outraged, an emotional Stevens called a number of senators and threatened to resign. Today, President Eisenhower stepped into the arena and delivered a clear warning to McCarthy by supporting Stevens to the hilt.

Aussies Welcome Queen

More than 500 small craft packed Sydney Harbour today and thousands of flag-waving citizens filled the water front as Queen Elizabeth sailed into Australian waters to begin the first-ever visit to the country by a reigning monarch. Standing on the bridge of their liner, *The Gothic,* both the Queen and the Duke of Edinburgh were clearly impressed and excited by their welcome, waving enthusiastically to boat-owners and those who had packed headlands around *The Gothic*'s berth at Atholl Bight.

Polio Vaccine Tests On Kids

A new anti-polio vaccine developed by American specialist Dr. Jonas Salk began a run of tests today in Pittsburgh when a group of school children were given doses.

Dr. Salk has refined his vaccine since March 1953 when he announced that he had vaccinated 161 adult and child volunteers with an encouraging drop in the level of antibodies in all subjects.

At that stage he said a practical vaccine for mass protection against the often-fatal disease was not yet available. The Pittsburgh trials suggest that is no longer the case.

Born this month:
2: Christie Brinkley,
US supermodel
18: John Travolta,
film actor, singer, dancer
20: Patty Hearst,
US newspaper empire
heiress
22: Ian Stark,
international showjumper

DEPARTURES

Died this month:
7: Maxwell Badenheim,
US novelist, poet,
playwright
17: Princess Marie-
Astrid, member of
Luxembourg royal family

FEBRUARY 4

Comets Fly Again

Less than a month after the second fatal crash of a
Comet airliner, BOAC today announced their seven-
strong fleet can fly once more.

The British international carrier says that 50
modifications their engineers have made to the aircraft
make the Comets completely safe and airworthy.

Report Finds Smoking-Cancer Link

There is a link between smoking and lung cancer, a standing committee investigating cancer and chemotherapy announced in London today. The Minister of Health warned against alarmist conclusions, pointing out that the report had not identified the agent responsible and had said work risks and atmospheric pollution may be causes.

Tobacco manufacturers claimed that their research had not proved that smoking caused cancer - it occurs in people who never smoke and only in a small proportion of those who do. Also, despite similar smoking habits, cancer is more prevalent in towns than in rural areas.

Egyptian Leaders In Power See-Saw

AFTER A WEEKEND WHICH SAW him sacked as President and placed under house arrest, General Neguib re-emerged as the strong man of the nation he has led since the 1952 coup which deposed King Farouk.

The 53 year old General's see-saw of fortune follows months of infighting among young officers of the Revolutionary Council, many of whom accused Neguib of wanting to be a dictator. When Neguib was arrested, they put 36 year old Colonel Gamal Nasser in charge.

Within hours, pro-Neguib demonstrations began country-wide. Cairo University campuses were closed after police killed at least 10 rioting students, and cavalry officers threatened to mutiny if Neguib was not reinstated.

Neguib reappeared as suddenly as he'd vanished, telling a welcoming crowd who'd gathered at the Revolution Palace that the weekend's events had been: 'Just a summer storm which, thank Allah, is now over.'

Strangely, the position of Colonel Nasser (pictured right), Neguib's Deputy PM and Minister of the Interior since June 1953, does not appear affected by the attempted coup. Observers say he is clearly a man to watch in coming months.

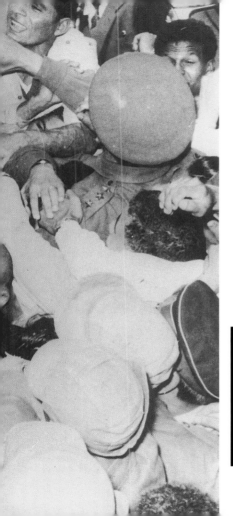

French Prepare For Dien Bien Phu Showdown

Intelligence reports today confirmed that North Vietnam's Viet Minh commander, General Giap, is gathering large units of his communist guerrilla forces to lay seige to the French-held South Vietnamese fort at Dien Bien Phu.

It is news the French army's commander, General Navarre, has been awaiting since his troops recaptured the fort last November. Since then, the strategic stronghold has been strengthened by an extensive fortification system and the Japanese-built airfield has been repaired. When the Viet Minh attack they will meet some of France's best soldiers, including paratroopers and Foreign Legionnaires. If General Giap's forces can recapture the airfield they will not only eliminate Navarre's ability to hit back from the air, but cut him off from all reinforcements except paratroops.

Archers Celebrate 800

Still being broadcast five times a week by the BBC and by far the world's longest-running radio 'soap' after more than 40 years, The Archers celebrated a relatively early milestone this day in 1954 with the broadcast of its 800th episode.

Introduced in 1951 as an entertaining device for passing information to British farmers, this 'everyday story of country folk' quickly captured the imaginations and loyalty of town-dwellers to give it a daily audience of 10 million - another world record.

WAR

H-Bomb Fall-out Burns Japanese Fishermen

THE HYDROGEN BOMB - a device 600 times more powerful than the atomic bombs which destroyed Hiroshima and Nagasaki in 1945 to bring World War II to an end - claimed its first human victims today when Japanese fishermen 70 miles from the test site were showered with radioactive dust.

Within days, all aboard their unfortunately-named boat, *Lucky Dragon,* were vomiting, experiencing dizziness and sunburn-like itching. Aware something was seriously wrong, the crew returned to Japan where all were hospitalized. By year end, all had incurable cancers. Tests showed *Lucky Dragon* to be saturated with radioactivity.

The strength of the explosion, triggered on the remote Bikini Atoll, took official US observers by surprise and overwhelmed scientific measuring instruments. Equivalent to 12 million pounds of TNT, it created a flash which the ill-fated fishermen described as 'a terrible light' which made it seem as if the sun was rising in the west.

Viet Minh Attack Dien Bien Phu

Communist Viet Minh troops today launched the largest offensive of their eight-year Indo-China war against French colonial forces when they began to lay seige to Dien Bien Phu.

The ferocity and strength of the Viet Minh attack suggests the North Vietnamese are prepared to sacrifice many infantry to capture the French stronghold. For their part, the French now have no way out except victory. Completely cut off from reinforcements, they cannot evacuate by air.

Stars To Be On 45

The days of the old 78 rpm record were numbered today when three of the world's leading recording companies - Columbia, Decca and MGM - announced they were following the early lead of RCA Victor, London and Capitol to switch future production to the new 45 and 33 rpm 'high fidelity' formats.

Although production of the fragile old 78s would continue for some years, the shape of pop music had changed forever.

Kenyans Seek Mau Mau Surrender

Attempts by the Kenyan and British governments to arrange a mass surrender of Mau Mau terrorists - mostly Kikuyu tribe members who have fought a bloody two-year war against white settlers in a bid for independence - were attacked today in the colony's Legislative Council.

Security forces, who scored a notable public relations victory on March 7 when they captured Mau Mau commanders 'General Katanga' and 'General Tanganyika', have been using a letter from a third captive, 'General China', to persuade other Mau Mau leaders that nothing will be gained by terrorism.

With the Mau Mau's mastermind Jomo 'Burning Spear' Kenyatta in captivity since November 1952, critics of the Kenyan government's initiative say that continued 'search-and-destroy' missions into the Kikuyu tribe's homelands are the only real solution.

MARCH 21

Third Man Theory – Kilby A Spy?

THE CORRIDORS of Whitehall were buzzing today following the leak of information that Harold 'Kim' Philby, the debonair First Secretary at the British Embassy in Washington, was being recalled to London for interrogation by MI6.

As the rumour mill went into overdrive, it became clear that Philby – a noted intellectual, friend of the rich and famous, and a one-time tip to become head of the MI6 intelligence team – is suspected of warning diplomats Guy Burgess and Donald Maclean in 1951, just as they were due to be arrested and charged with being Soviet spies.

Burgess and Maclean disappeared in June 1951, despite an international hunt. In September 1953 Maclean's wife and family vanished from their home in Geneva, Switzerland. All are believed to be in the Soviet Union, though this has yet to be proved.

MARCH 5

UK To Get Commercial TV

A good-news month for British TV viewers tired of a BBC monopoly and a one-channel choice of programmes. A second channel, funded by on-air advertising, has been given the go-ahead.

First announced last year, the government-sponsored Television Bill was finally introduced on March 5. Despite strong opposition from members of the socialist Labour Party who saw commercial TV as a big-business rip-off, MPs approved its introduction in 1956.

The new service is scheduled to commence in London, with a Birmingham-based station following.

The sting in this tale? On March 1 the government hiked the annual cost of a TV license from £2 to £3.

MARCH 27

National Deaths Spark Inquiry

Long the subject of controversy, Britain's annual Grand National steeplechase became the subject of an official inquiry today when four horses were killed in a race won by *Royal Tan*.

Opponents of the 30-fence, four-and-a-half mile race claim it is too hard on horses and riders who travel from all over the world to the Aintree Racecourse in Liverpool. In 1951 only three of the 33 entries managed to finish.

Fervour As Billy Graham Touches Down

London was hit by religion this spring as American evangelist Billy Graham mounted his first British crusade.

With a fervent charismatic style unlike anything they'd seen in English churches, Graham drew thousands to London's Harringay Arena this month to hear him preach.

In May, the man who would become a valued friend and adviser to successive American presidents had a triumphant end to his crusade when 180,000 packed Wembley Stadium.

WATERFRONT MAKES CONTENDER BRANDO FOURTH-TIME CHAMP

t had to come eventually, and it finally did this year after three successive unsuccessful nominations. Marlon Brando was declared Best Actor in this year's Academy Awards ceremony for his powerful performance in the movie which also won the Best Picture Oscar, produced one for director Elia Kazan, a Supporting Actress statuette for Eva Marie Saint, and another - for Story and Screenplay - for Budd Schulberg.

On The Waterfront was a remarkable success story all round, for it also won Supporting Actor nominations for Rod Steiger, Lee J. Cobb and Karl Malden, and three more Oscars (for black and white cinematography, editing and art direction) for Boris Kaufman, Gene Milford and Richard Day, respectively.

Behind its gritty story of betrayal in the midst of an often-bloody war between striking dock workers and their bosses, was the ironic fact that both director and writer had named names to Senator Joe McCarthy's House Un-American Activities Committee, thereby consigning many erstwhile friends and colleagues to blacklisted exile and years of struggle.

Whether this irony helped the noted-liberal Brando pull the last ounce of pathos from his role or not, it was a *tour de force* performance which saw off the challenge of Humphrey Bogart's manic Captain Queeg in *The Caine Mutiny,* Bing Crosby (in *The Country Girl),* James Mason (in *A Star Is Born)* and Dan O'Herlihy (for *The Adventures of Robinson Crusoe).*

Grace Kelly was a revelation as the wife of an alcoholic in *The Country Girl,* so no-one begrudged her the Best Actress Oscar she won in the face of competition from Judy Garland *(A Star Is Born),* Dorothy Dandridge *(Carmen Jones),* 1953's *Roman Holiday* winner Audrey Hepburn (for *Sabrina)* and Jane Wyman (for *Magnificent Obsession).*

The Best Picture contest won by *On the Waterfront* saw it beat off *The Caine Mutiny* and *The Country Girl,* along with the all-singin' all-dancin' *Seven Brides For Seven Brothers,* and the romantic comedy *Three Coins In The Fountain.* The musical had to make do with Best Musical Score awards for Saul Chaplin and Adolph Deutsch, while *Three Coins In The Fountain* produced Original Song trophies for Sammy Cahn and Jule Styne and the Color Cinematography

Marlon Brandon and Rod Steiger in On The Waterfront

Cinematography award for Milton Krasner.

Alfred Hitchcock did win a Best Director nomination for *Rear Window,* though many were surprised that James Stewart's excellent performance in that didn't get him similarly short-listed. Given the absence of *Sabrina* from the Best Picture nominations (although it gave Edith Head her sixth Costume Design Award), it was surprising that Billy Wilder should have won a Director mention. Same goes for William Wellman, whose *The High And The Mighty* delivered only a Supporting Actress nomination for Claire Trevor, although it won Dimitri Tiomkin an Oscar for his score.

But the year, and the headlines, belonged to Marlon Brando. His performance and eventual recognition were almost universally acclaimed. Typically, he didn't bother to attend the ceremony which acknowledged his genius.

APRIL

Haley Starts To Rock

The future of popular music was changed forever today at the New York studios of Decca Records when a former country and western singer did his manager a favour and recorded a new version of a song first written and produced unsuccessfully 18 months earlier.

The singer was 29 year old Bill Haley. The manager was Dave Myers. The song was, of course, *Rock Around The Clock*, written by Tin Pan Alley veterans Max Freedman and Jimmy DeKnight and previously covered by Myers with a girl singer, Sunny Dae.

When first released, Haley's new version sold only moderately, and nowhere near as well as his previous single *Crazy Man, Crazy*, which had been a Top 20 hit. But its use over the credits of the 1955 film *The Blackboard Jungle* would make it a worldwide smash, help create the whole rock 'n' roll revolution, and go on to sell more than 25 million copies.

Third Comet Falls To Earth

THE BRITISH GOVERNMENT today ordered the immediate grounding of all BOAC Comets and withdrew their airworthiness certificates following a third fatal crash yesterday, 35 miles north of the Mediterranean island of Stromboli.

All 14 passengers and seven crew aboard the Rome-Johannesburg flight died when the Comet fell into the sea shortly after take-off. It is believed it was flying through a storm when disaster struck.

As a massive hunt for wreckage and bodies began in the Mediterranean, BOAC chairman Sir Miles Thomas told press: 'We have had three inexplicable tragedies. They all follow a certain pattern on reaching or approaching maximum altitude at full power'.

One of the first ships to reach the crash area was the aircraft carrier HMS *Eagle*.

It recovered five bodies, with others being found by local fishermen working by the light of flares dropped by aircraft.

Full-scale tests of destruction are to be carried out on a Comet at the Royal Aircraft Establishment in Farnborough, Hampshire. Whatever they prove, confidence in the world's first jet airliner is so low, it's hard to see how it can survive.

New Trials For Polio

New York's National Foundation for Infantile Paralysis today took on the task of overseeing independent nationwide tests for the polio vaccine developed and trialed by Dr. Jonas Salk. The tests will be organized and evaluated by Dr. Thomas Francis Jr, of the University of Michigan's School of Public Health.

The year-long trial will consist of 'blind' tests using Salk's vaccine and placebo injections, to be given under a coding system to ensure that final results will not be known until the end of the exercise.

Delays in producing enough vaccine samples to begin the trials were solved by the University of Toronto, main 'growers' of the virus. Their team has succeeded in devizing new, more effective and safe ways of killing the polio bug to make the vaccine available in quantity.

Nasser Ousts Neguib

Colonel Gamal Nasser has emerged as Egypt's new Prime Minister, ousting President Neguib in a bloodless coup to end a seven-week struggle for power.

The 36 year old victor used Neguib's absence from Cairo - for a goodwill trip to Sudan - to arrest his main supporters and organize anti-Neguib demonstrations.

Neguib will remain President, but as a powerless figurehead - the role originally intended for him when young army officers used him as a front for their ejection of King Farouk.

ARRIVALS

Born this month:

1: Giancarlo Antognoni, Italian football star

4: Gary Moore, Irish blues guitarist, singer, songwriter (Thin Lizzy, Skid Row)

5: Stan (Stannard) Ridgway, US rock singer, songwriter

8: John Schneider, US actor *(Dukes of Hazzard)*, country music singer

9: Denis Quaid, US actor *(The Right Stuff, Great Balls of Fire)*; brother of Randy, husband of Meg Ryan

17: Riccardo Patrese, Italian Formula 1 racing driver

19: Trevor Francis, English international football player, manager

DEPARTURES

Died this month:

10: Auguste-Marie-Louis Lumière, French cinema pioneer

17: Theodore Komisarjevsky, theatre director

25: Joseph Hergesheimer, US novelist

Vietnam: US Warns China

Confronted by intelligence reports proving that China is actively aiding the communist Viet Minh forces of North Vietnamese commander General Giap in their assault on the French garrison at Dien Bien Phu, US Secretary of State John Foster Dulles today warned the Chinese to keep out of the conflict.

Describing the potential loss of Indo-China as a 'terrible disaster', he called on Western powers for a united front which should decrease the need for united action.

Troops Crack Down On Mau Mau

WITH THEIR 'GENERAL CHINA' surrender plan an admitted failure, the Kenyan government hit back this morning when a strike force of British and Kenyan troops descended on settlements near Nairobi to round up tens of thousands of suspected Mau Mau terrorists and their supporters.

Just before dawn, 5,000 troops, 1,000 armed police and hundreds of government-loyal Kikuyu Home Guards moved in to arrest about 40,000 suspects and take half of them away to camps for interrogation.

The surrender scheme was abandoned after security forces waited 11 days for negotiators to arrive at a rendezvous in the Aberdare Mountains foothills. When one left a message alleging that Mau Mau were threatening to kill intermediaries and asking for 'sky-shouting aircraft' - planes with loudspeakers - to warn that no-one should be killed for negotiating, the decision to act more decisively was taken.

APRIL

APRIL 4

Toscanini Drops Baton

The tempestuous Arturo Toscanini conducted his very last concert tonight at New York's Carnegie Hall and entered retirement at the age of 87. Fittingly, the farewell saw him leading The NBC Symphony Orchestra, the team created for him in 1937 when he fled Mussolini's fascist Italy for a new life in the US. Typically, the irascible and notoriously-temperamental maestro did not take a final bow. He merely dropped his baton and walked off-stage, not even returning to acknowledge a lengthy standing ovation.

APRIL 29

Ike Snubs A-Bomb Chief

President Eisenhower today defended his recent decision to withdraw security clearance for scientist Robert Oppenheimer (pictured), leader of the Manhattan Project team which developed the atomic bomb in 1945.

Oppenheimer's access to top-secret data was withdrawn on December 23, 1953 when it was alleged that he had associated with communists and delayed the development of the hydrogen bomb.

While the scientist, who now heads the Institute for Advanced Study in Princeton, New Jersey, has admitted the former charge, he denies the latter.

MAY

IBM Herald Dawn Of Computer Age

An announcement by the American-based International Business Machines Corporation (IBM) today gave the first indications of new advances which would go on to revolutionize the world's workplaces.

IBM revealed its development of a business machine said to be capable of making 10 million arithmetical calculations an hour, using cathode ray memory tubes and data stored on magnetic tapes. Each machine is claimed to be able to hold as much information as the phone directory of a large city

So far, IBM have agreed to rent out 30 of the new machines, although deliveries of their 'electronic brain' will not commence until 1955 when a typical installation is expected to cost customers $25,000 (£8,000) a month.

Boeing Enter Jet Airliner Race

With all BOAC Comets still grounded after three mysterious crashes, American plane-builders Boeing has entered the potentially massive passenger jet airliner market with a formidable challenge. The Seattle-based corporation today unveiled its first salvo in its bid for world domination – the prototype of its Boeing 707.

Bannister Breaks Four-Minute Mile

ONE OF THE WORLD'S most formidable and sought-after athletic targets - the sub four-minute mile - was achieved today when Roger Bannister, a 25 year old British medical student, broke the tape at an Oxford University track in a world-beating time of 3 mins 59.4 secs.

Bannister's victory, in a match between Oxford University and the Amateur Athletic Association, was also a triumph over his two closest rivals for the first four-minute mile - American Wes Santee and Australian John Landy.

Santee's bid had ended when he was disqualified from amateur competition, while Landy would beat Bannister's time by more than a second in June to prove how close he'd been to being first.

Racing in a chill wind which had threatened the record attempt, Bannister's early pacemakers were fellow graduates Chris Chataway and Chris Brasher. Their efforts still left Bannister needing to cover the last quarter-mile lap in 59 seconds to break both the nine-year record of Sweden's Gunder Haegg and that magic four-minute barrier.

Always a dedicated doctor first and an athlete second, Bannister would retire from racing by year-end to concentrate on his medical career.

Teds No Threat, Says Minister

One of the most striking British fashion developments in recent times has been the emergence of 'teddy boys' - gangs of youths who've adopted a distinctive dress code which incorporates long Edwardian-style jackets (hence the 'teddy'), skinny drainpipe pants and a hairstyle with long sideburns.

Collecting on street corners and around the new fashionable coffee-bars, the 'teds' pose an imagined threat to older nervous folk and British newspapers have been quick to report their fears.

Home Secretary David Maxwell-Fyfe entered the debate today. While he acknowledged people's concerns, he said the problem was not widespread and was, in any case, containable.

More Mau Mau Snared

The Kenyan government's crackdown on the Mau Mau shows no sign of let-up.

As news continues to come in of new operations, including jet fighter flights over forest areas believed to contain Kikuyu guerrillas, another mass arrest exercise near Nairobi today saw a further 10,000 suspects detained.

On May 26 the Mau Mau hit back with a strategically-unimportant but invaluable public relations coup when they attacked and burned down Kenya's famous Treetops Hotel, the safari centre occupied by Princess Elizabeth in 1952 when she learned she'd become Queen on the death of her father, King George VI.

MAY 8

France Mourns As Viet Minh Take Dien Bien Phu

FRENCH RADIO STATIONS played solemn music and public places of entertainment closed in respect today as news came in of a Viet Minh victory in the 55-day siege of Dien Bien Phu. The entire French garrison - around 16,000 crack troops, including 3,000 paratroop reinforcements - is either been killed or captured.

Only one post, called 'Isabelle' and about three miles from the main stronghold, continues to hold out. Its capture is inevitable since the North Vietnamese communist forces over-ran the last French defenses after an all-night battle.

As the Viet Minh launched their last successful attack, the local commander, Brigadier General de Castries radio-telephoned French headquarters in Hanoi. His dramatic call said: 'We can no longer do anything. We will not surrender. They're a few metres away...now they're everywhere!'

The commander's last-known action was to order heavy artillery gunners at 'Isabelle' to fire on his command post if the Viet Minh broke through. There has been no news of the General since, nor of the only woman at Dien Bien Phu, the medical worker Mlle de Galard Terraube .

A French government call for an immediate truce was tabled at the UN-sponsored Geneva peace conference which had begun on May 3, but on May 10 the Viet Minh made their intentions clear by rejecting the proposal and demanding freedom for Vietnam, Cambodia and Laos.

MAY 8

BBC Bans Ray's Raunchy Hit

Shutting the stable door long after the horse had bolted, governors of the British Broadcasting Corporation today banned any future airtime for American singer Johnnie Ray's (pictured right) sexy Such A Night - but only after it became the UK's best-selling single.

The BBC said it was reacting to complaints about the song's dubious lyrics and Ray's suggestive grunts and groans.

Their ban, and the resultant publicity, only helped to lodge Such A Night at No 1 for eight weeks. American radio bans had been introduced on the record's release and it sank without trace there, although a version by The Drifters reached No 5 in the rhythm 'n' blues charts

Supreme Court Outlaws Segregated Schools

Conservatives reacted angrily today to a US Supreme Court ruling which outlaws segregated education for some 8.5 million white and 2.5 million black children attending schools in southern states.

Chief Justice Earl Warren's judgment, which overturns an 1896 ruling that education could be 'separate but equal', said separated educational facilities were 'inherently unequal'.

Negative reactions to the Supreme Court's decision have been expected since hearings on segregation began in December 1953 and today's announcement was widely anticipated.

Typical of the condemnations were those of Mississippi's Senator Eastland, who proclaimed: 'The South will not abide by nor obey this legislative decision by a political court'. Georgia's Agricultural Commissioner Linder warned: 'We are going to have segregation, regardless of what the court rules'.

The battle lines were drawn.

JUNE

18 Year Old Piggott Makes Racing History

Legendary British jockey Lester Piggott entered the history books today when, at the age of only 18, he became the youngest-ever rider to win the English Derby classic on the American-bred *Never Say Die.*

The colt, which book-makers had made a rank 33-1 outsider, also made history by being the first US horse to win Britain's leading flat race since *Iriquois* took the honours in 1881.

Piggott, who won his first major race at the age of 13, had come second in the 1952 Derby, and would go on to win it many times more during a distinguished victory-packed career in Britain, France, Hong Kong and the US

Pope Launches Eurovision Network

POPE PIUS XII APPEARED SIMULTANEOUSLY on TV screens in Britain, France, West Germany, Switzerland, Belgium, Holland, Denmark and - of course - Italy tonight to launch the Eurovision network, an experimental exchange between leading national television companies.

As exchanges continue and become more regular, its creators have a long-term vision of a trans-European link to speed news communication, share production costs of international sports events and break down the artificial barriers between participating countries.

Pope Pius touched on that aspect during his Eurovision début, saying that he hoped the new technology would 'let the nations learn to know each other better'.

Today's inaugural exercise, which included coverage of the annual flower festival in Montreux, Switzerland, involved a complex 4,000 mile chain of linking relays.

BBC plans their contribution to the next link-up to include coverage of a Glasgow police sports meeting and the Trooping the Colours ceremony to mark the Queen's official birthday.

ARRIVALS
Born this month:

2: Dan Bill, Canadian pop singer, songwriter

11: John Dyson, Australian cricketer

13: Jorge Santana, US-Mexican rock guitarist (Malo), brother of Carlos; Robert Donaldson, US rock pianist, trumpeter (Bo Donaldson & The Heywoods)

14: Maureen Nolan, Irish singer, dancer (The Nolans)

15: Terri Gibbs, US country singer, songwriter

16: Gary Roberts, Irish rock guitarist, singer (The Boomtown Rats)

20: Alan Lamb, English cricketer

25: David Paich, US rock musician, singer, songwriter (Toto)

NEWS IN BRIEF

1: While a hearing found atom scientist Dr Robert Oppenheimer 'loyal and discreet', his security clearance was denied

15: Dr Edward Teller told the Washington Oppenheimer enquiry that the H-bomb development was slowed by Oppenheimer's lack of moral support

16: Oppenheimer's successor denied the H-bomb could have been made any earlier

JUNE 18

Mendes-France Becomes French PM

With his country still reeling from their army's humiliating and overwhelming defeat at Dien Bien Phu and the Geneva truce talks bogged down by mutual distrust, Pierre Mendes-France made no secret of his intention to negotiate a Vietnamese peace treaty as he lobbied to become France's new prime minister.

His honesty and pragmatism paid off today when a majority of French members of the National Assembly voted him into the post, telling him to figure out a way of getting France out of Vietnam with no loss of face. He also has to extricate France from increasingly troublesome relationships with Morocco and Tunisia, its long-time north African colonies.

JUNE 15

McCarthy Digs CIA Hole

Senator Joe McCarthy began to dig an even deeper hole for himself this month, coming up against President Eisenhower once more to raise a question mark over his chairmanship of the Senate's Un-American Activities Committee.

On June 2, the Wisconsin firebrand acted true to form when he alleged serious infiltration of the CIA and America's nuclear weapons plants. As usual, his allegations were strong on rhetoric and bluster but weak on supporting evidence.

President Eisenhower was not prepared to let McCarthy drag his intelligence community through the mire of unsubstantiated accusation and public vilification he'd inflicted on senior military figures in February.

On June 6 Ike announced he would not allow McCarthy to investigate the CIA.

JUNE 12

It's Raining...Frogs?!

Weather-fixated Britain had a real treat today when a large crowd watching a naval cadet display at Sutton Park, Birmingham found themselves drenched in a rain shower which included thousands of frogs.

Meteorologists could only cite historical precedents for what was, by all accounts, a pretty slimy experience. The whys and wherefores went unanswered.

They could explain the complete darkness which covered Britain on June 30. A complete solar eclipse emptied schools and offices as people gathered to watch the moon block out the sun's rays.

Ike And Churchill Set Peace Agenda

PRESIDENT EISENHOWER and British Prime Minister Sir Winston Churchill today ended a weekend summit in Washington by signing what they have named The Potomac Agreement – a document which cements 'the intimate comradeship' of their two nations in a united pursuit of world peace and international justice.

Both leaders used the signing ceremony to reinforce what the Prime Minister described as 'the unbroken and unbreakable unity of the Anglo-American world', generally recognized by observers as a clear warning to Eastern bloc leaders of a continued almost unconditional alliance.

Behind the scenes there had been uneasy talks about French Indo-China between US Secretary of State John Foster Dulles and British Foreign Secretary Anthony Eden.

Both appear to have accepted that Vietnam will have to be partitioned, creating a communist northern half and a southern portion which the West will have to support – and defend, if the Ho Chi Minh regime ever moves to cancel the new borders.

The summit was a suitably high note on which to end a memorable month for the Prime Minister. Earlier, he'd become Sir Winston Churchill when he was invested with The Order of the Garter, Britain's highest level of knighthood, by Queen Elizabeth.

SPORT

GERMANY DEFEAT UNBEATABLE HUNGARY

Hungary's apparently-unbeatable soccer stars, including ace strikers Puskas, Kocsis and Hidegkuti, arrived in Switzerland for the 1954 World Cup so far ahead in everyone's books the only serious betting was on which of the other 15 participating nations they'd meet - and defeat - in the final.

In their opening pool games the Hungarians confirmed their superiority by smashing nine goals past Korea and eight against Germany. The second match contained warnings for Hungary, however, as the Germans scored three times in reply and Puskas was kicked out of the tournament by centre-half Werner Liebrich.

Hungary cruised into the quarter-finals - where they beat Brazil 4-2 in an horrific brawl which saw three players dismissed and dressing-room fights after the game - while the Germans had to win a pool play-off with Turkey before beating Yugoslavia 2-0 to win a semi-final place against Austria.

While the Hungarian forwards maintained their formidable superiority by scoring four goals against Uruguay in the semi-final, their once-impenetrable defense was beaten twice. Ominously, the Germans only allowed Austria a single consolation goal as they pumped six past their hapless keeper.

Sentiment got the better of Hungary's coach and the still-injured Puskas returned to lead his team out. While he overcame his ankle damage enough to give Hungary an early lead which Czibor doubled within eight minutes, Puskas was a comparative passenger unable to do anything as Morlock replied for Germany and Rahn drew the game level before half time.

It was Rahn who, only seven minutes from time, belted in the goal which gave Germany a famous and completely unexpected world championship.

MOTOR RACING
FANGIO SUPREME AS FORMULA ONE RETURNS

After two seasons of Formula Two racing while the major teams concentrated on creating a new generation of machines, the World Drivers' Championship returned to Formula One in 1954 with 2.5 litre engines and dramatically-altered streamlined bodies the order of the day for Ferrari, Maserati and Mercedes.

It was Juan Fangio's new Mercedes W196 which powered him to victory in four of the six races he entered after starting the season driving the new Maserati 250F, and gave him the 1954 world champion title.

Engines also dominated the Indy 500 - specifically the four-cylinder Offenhausers - the 'Offy'. Uniquely, all 33 cars on the grid were Offy powered, but it was reigning 500 champ Bill Vukovich's Kurtis-Offy KK500A which won the annual classic.

The 1954 US motor racing season was especially notable for Lee Perry who, in addition to winning the Daytona Beach and road race in a Chrysler, also became NASCAR champion.

But the year ended sadly. On October 30, the racing fraternity was stunned to learn of the death, in a private plane crash, of Wilbur Shaw, the 52 year old President of the Indianapolis Speedway and three-time winner of the 500.

GOLF
THOMSON WAVES AUSSIE FLAG

Australian golf came of age this year with the emergence of Peter Thomson, 24 year old winner of the British Open - the first Aussie victory in a major - and Peter Toogood ending the year as the world's leading amateur.

Proving his Royal Birkdale win over Bobby Locke, Dai Rees and Sid Scott was no fluke, Thomson partnered Kel Nagle to help Australia beat Argentina in the second Canada Cup tournament at Montreal's Laval-sur-Lac course, and emerged triumphant in the Professional Match Play championship.

Australia's trophy-filled season also included a British Amateur victory at Muirfield by Doug Bachli, a Melbourne club-mate of Thomson, an Australian team win at St. Andrews in the Commonwealth Tournament, and the capture of the St. George's Cup at Sandwich by Harry Berwick.

Morlock slides the ball in to begin Germany's comeback victory over Hungary.

Vietnam Divided In French Peace Pact

VIETNAM, THE ASIAN COUNTRY wracked by a bloody war between communist Viet Minh guerrillas and occupying French colonial forces, was split in two today under the terms of a treaty hammered out in Geneva by the new French prime minister, Pierre Mendes-France.

The communist regime led by the exiled revolutionary Ho Chi Minh will control that half of Vietnam north of the 17th Parallel, while the puppet government of Emperor Bao Dai will rule the southern half with continued French support.

Smoothing out of the remaining disagreements were hastened by a midnight deadline imposed by Mendes-France during talks at La Bocage, a villa used as headquarters for the French delegation. While he clearly believes he's achieved his objective of reaching an honorable settlement, the deal has some critics.

Senator Knowland, Republican leader in the US Senate, said the Geneva deal would be considered 'a considerable victory for communism' throughout the Far East and prophesied the West would come to regret that such an agreement had been 'forced upon the French'. There will also be no joint guarantee signed by the Geneva Conference powers - the US will declare that it won't upset an agreement it can respect, the other eight will confine their support to verbal statements at a plenary session.

At the end of the month, Mendes-France would begin his attempt to solve France's problems in Morocco and Tunisia, where nationalists are demanding independence.

JULY 1

Defector Petrov Names Tass Spies

In the Australian capital Canberra, defector diplomat Vladimir Petrov told an espionage commission that all journalists working for TASS, the Soviet news agency, were spies reporting to the KGB. Petrov, who surrendered to Australian intelligence officers in April, had already exposed a Soviet spy ring and confirmed that British diplomats Burgess and Maclean had fled to Moscow when they vanished in 1951.

COOKING FATS INCLUDING LARD AND DRIPPING 23

COOKING INCL LAR DRI

COOKING FATS INCLUDING LARD AND DRIPPING 24

COOK INC LAR DRI 2

PAGE 5.

Consumer's Name (BLOCK)

Address (BLOCK LETTERS)

COOKING FATS INCLUDING LARD AND DRIPPING 26

COOK! INCL LARD DRI 2

COOKING FATS INCLUDING LARD AND DRIPPING 25

COOKI INCL LARD DRIF 2

PAGE 5.—COOKING FAT

Consumer's Name..........
(BLOCK LETTERS)

Address..........
(BLOCK LETTERS)
Date.

Name & Address
of Retailer ....

JULY 2

Drobny Wins Longest-Ever Wimbledon

Long before the tie-break was introduced to settle drawn tennis matches, players were used to games going on, and on...and on. Even by the standards of 1954, today's mammoth Wimbledon final battle between the 32 year old Czech-born, Egyptian national Joroslav Drobny and Australia's Ken Rosewall, was memorable.

In the longest-ever final, Drobny overcame a bad knee injury and the brilliance of Rosewall to win by a remarkable 13-11, 4-6, 6-2, 9-7.

Their battle all but eclipsed the third successive Ladies win of America's Maureen 'Little Mo' Connolly, still only 20 but too much for the challenge of Althea Brough.

JULY 2

Britain Burns Ration Books

Ration books were torn up and burned all over Britain today as the government announced the end of all rationing after 14 years. London's Trafalgar Square was the scene of a mass ceremonial destruction of the hated coupons which restricted how much meat - the last commodity to be rationed - each citizen could buy.

For the first time since the start of WWII, the capital's Smithfield Market opened for business at midnight, with meat dealers describing the quality of deliveries as 'extraordinarily good'.

With butchers predicting price rises, members of the National Federation of Housewives began patrolling shops, threatening protests if prices did not fall.

JULY 27

British Troops To Quit Suez Canal Zone

TWO YEARS AFTER BRITISH forces invaded and seized control of the strategic Suez Canal Zone following a call by Egypt's King Farouk for all foreign nationals to quit the area, all 65,000 UK troops and airmen are to be pulled out of their bases by the end of 1956.

Under the terms of a deal negotiated with the Egyptian leader, Colonel Nasser, British arms and equipment will be 'mothballed' and the base maintained by Egyptian civilians. The 18,000 men of The King's African Rifles will also leave the Canal Zone, which has experienced British forces for 75 years.

Britain does retain the right to re-activate the base if Turkey or an Arab state is attacked, but the deal is a clear victory for Nasser and the other young officers who overthrew King Farouk in 1952 with the stated intention of ejecting what they described as 'Imperialist British forces' from Egyptian soil.

JULY 4

Germany Beat Hungary In World Cup

Soccer's World Cup lived up to its reputation for humbling favourites in Switzerland today when Hungary, generally acknowledged as the world's best, were beaten 3-2 by a West German team which had to fight back from being 2-0 down early in the Berne final. The West Germans had strolled to a 6-1 semi-final win over Austria. Their saviour in the final was star forward Rahn, who scored both the equalizer just before half-time, and the winner six minutes before the game's end.
(See Sports pages for full story)

JULY 15

Boeing 707 Takes Flight

The United States became the second member of the world's new jet air transport club today when its rival to the British Comet - the Boeing 707 - made its maiden flight from Seattle.

Incorporating many developments of Boeing's jet bomber programme and funded largely by the US Air Force to use in tanker form as an in-flight re-fueler, the four-engined 707 features engines slung individually beneath its 130-feet wings to ensure continued power if fire or failure affects any one.

Boeing's new baby will be able to carry 219 passengers at a top speed of more than 600 mph (almost 1000 kph).

JULY 1

Virus Wipes Out Rabbits

British ecologists today warned that myxomatosis, the killer virus which first took hold in Kent last year, is set to wipe out the entire rabbit population. Up to 90 per cent of burrows in the south of England are believed to be infected.

Deliberately introduced from Australia, where it was developed to tackle that country's rabbit infestation problem, myxomatosis is considered necessary by farmers who lose about £50 million worth of crops a year to rabbits. Environmentalists claim the disappearance of rabbits will impact on the balance of nature with terrible long-term implications.

Truck Driver Makes Record

Not the kind of headline guaranteed to stop readers in their tracks, agreed. But the benefit of hindsight's a wonderful thing.

The truck driver was a 19 year old Elvis Presley, and the record was his distinctive version of That's All Right Mama, a song written by blues singer Arthur 'Big Boy' Crudup.

Recorded by Presley in the Memphis studios of Sun Records, it combined a driving country-style arrangement with a near-black vocal style to break every musical rule in the book - and step firmly over the line in a fiercely-segregated South.

One of the most remarkable, influential and controversial performing artists in history had arrived.

JULY

Two Chinas Return To Centre Of World Stage

THE STRUGGLE BETWEEN the two Chinas - the Communist regime of Mao Tse-Tung which controls the vast mainland country, and the Nationalist government of General Chiang Kai-Shek based on the island of Formosa (Taiwan) - may have vanished from the front pages while other world events dominated headlines. But it leaped back to international prominence this month as fresh hostilities broke out to signal a fresh round of military action.

First indications came on August 9 when a naval action off the Formosan coast near Taipei ended in a Nationalist triumph and the sinking of eight Communist gunboats.

The arrival in Beijing, Communist China's capital, of a British Labour Party delegation on August 14, could have indicated a slight thaw in Mao's ice-cold attitude to the West. In the event, not even the skills of Labour leader Clement Attlee, a noted negotiator, could make any impression on the Communists.

On August 17, President Eisenhower did nothing to calm things down when he committed the US 7th Fleet to the region. His move was designed to send a clear 'no-invasion of Formosa at any costs' warning to Mao. Seven days later Ike confirmed his hatred of socialism when he outlawed the American Communist Party.

All Calm As UN Quits Korea

The United Nations Command officially left Korea today to mark the end of a bloody three year war in which UN forces had taken to the battlefield for the first time since the organization's birth in 1945.

A year after a ceasefire deal was signed at Panmunjon, Korea returned to being a nation split between implacably hostile regimes - Chinese-backed communists in the north, and a pro-western Republic in the South. The war began in June 1950 when North Korean forces swept over the 39th Parallel border in a surprise attack. They almost overran South Korea before an American-led UN force landed to begin a recapture of lost territory.

Truce Signed

STARS AND STRIPES

Iran Gives Britain £238 Million For Oil

The three-year row between Britain and Iran, begun in March 1951 when the Iranian government attempted to seize all assets of the Anglo-Iranian Oil Company, ended fairly amicably today with a deal which gives Britain £238 million ($700m) in reparation for the nationalization of Iran's oil industry.

Britain had been involved in the development of Iran's oilfields since 1909, but the growth of Islamic fundamentalism and Iranian nationalism led to a series of bloody riots, a number of deaths in the British community, and numerous changes of government before the Shah of Iran was able to regain control of events in August 1953 and commence negotiations with Britain.

NEWS IN BRIEF

1: The British Atomic Energy Authority was established in London

4: In Britain, the maiden flight of the UK's first supersonic fighter, the English Electric built P-1 Lightning; Sir Kenneth Clark appointed chairman of Britain's new Independent Television Authority

10: Retirement of champion jockey Sir Gordon Richards; Holland and former colony Indonesia severed their last political ties in The Hague

22: Victory in the Swiss Grand Prix gave Argentina's Juan Fangio the world motor racing championship

31: Surrey became English County Cricket Champions for the third year in succession

ARRIVALS

Born this month:

1: Sammy McIlroy, Northern Irish international football star

26: James Wallace, Scottish politician

27: John Lloyd, British Davis Cup tennis player, former husband of Chris Evert

DEPARTURES

Died this month:

3: Colette (Sidonie-Gabrielle Colette), French novelist

24: Getulio Dornelles Varga, Brazilian president, resigned amid corruption charges, then committed suicide

AUGUST 26

Tolkien Publishes Ring Saga

British bookshops took delivery today of three books which would become immediate highly-acclaimed best-sellers and go on to cause a revolution in fantasy literature.

Published simultaneously, *The Fellowship Of The Ring*, *The Two Towers* and *Return Of The King* formed the saga known as *The Lord Of The Rings*. Written by an Oxford University professor JRR Tolkien (pictured), they fused elements of Norse, Teutonic and Celtic myth to create a fictional world battled over by the forces of good and evil for control of a powerful magic ring.

Long-awaited sequels to Tolkien's *The Hobbit*, a cult classic since its publication in 1937, they would all become required reading for anyone with pretensions to hippiedom in the 1960s, spawn hundreds of pale imitations and a huge merchandizing empire.

AUGUST 28

Palmer Wins First Title

A young American golfer took the Detroit Country Club course on today in the 36-hole final of the US Amateur Championship to register his first career win in a national event. The newcomer was 24 year-old Arnold Palmer, from Latrobe, Ohio. Educated at Wake Forest and playing out of Pine Ridge, Ohio, he beat Robert Sweeny on the 36th hole of a tightly-contested match in an Amateur which was the first to imitate pro tournaments by roping off the fairways.

France Offers Colonies Self-Government

STUCK BETWEEN the rock of Moroccan and Tunisian demands for independence and the hard place of French conservatism, Prime Minister Pierre Mendes-France today tried to steer a compromise course by offering the two north African colonies an initial autonomy.

Mendes-France had flown to Tunis for final talks before making his offer of self-government. This meets some of the objectives of local nationalists without giving them the full independence French conservatives believe will lead to the loss of valuable colonial interests.

It proved enough for Mendes-France to win approval in a key National Assembly vote in Paris. But it was not enough for Moroccan nationalists. As riots spread across the colony, they called for the return of Sidi Mohammed Ben Youssef, the former Sultan of Morocco deposed and exiled by France in 1953.

Bannister Triumph, Peters Disaster In Canadian Games

A day of high drama in Vancouver, where the Empire and Commonwealth Games ended with a triumph-and-disaster scenario worthy of a Hollywood script.

The triumph came in what the organizers billed as the 'Mile of the Century' - a race between the only two athletes to have run sub four-minute miles, Briton Roger Bannister and Australia's John Landy.

Honours were taken by Bannister, who cannily tracked Landy throughout the race before out-manouevering him around the last bend and outpacing him along the finishing straight.

With the stadium still buzzing, marathon leader Jim Peters entered the stadium some 15 minutes ahead of his closest rival. Clearly exhausted by the 80-degree heat, the British champion began to lurch from side to side. Less than 200 yards from the finishing line, with the huge crowd silent, he staggered and fell onto the cinder track.

As onlookers wept, medical staff rushed to give Peters oxygen before rushing him to hospital, where he made a full recovery.

'54 No Calamity For Doris Day

No stranger to the British charts, perennially winsome girl-next-door Doris Day enjoyed a bonanza year of it in 1954, thanks to three songs taken from her hit movie *Calamity Jane*. In all, she spent a total of 43 weeks in the UK Top 20 to reinforce her position as one of Britain's all-time favourite Americans.

First to emerge was the heart-wrenching *Secret Love* which entered the chart at number 3 in April, lodged at the top for two months and enjoyed no less than 29 weeks in the Top 20. While that continued to reign supreme, the former Doris Kappelhoff's *Deadwood Stage* was released to begin a seven-week Top 20 stay.

Not content with that, in August - and with *Secret Love* still in the Top 10 she began another seven-week Top 20 run with *Black Hills Of Dakota* which included a couple of weeks in the Top 10.

Between 1952 and 1964, Doris Day would score 18 Top 30 hits in Britain, and return to number 1 in 1956 with *Que Sera, Sera (Whatever Will Be, Will Be)*. Her last big smash, the 1964 million-seller theme song from her movie *Move Over Darling*, would become a British hit all over again in 1987, this time adopted by the local gay community.

KIDDY CHOIR START INTERNATIONAL WANDERING FEVER

It's one of the strangest success stories in the history of pop, a field renowned for the unusual, and it goes like this: In the autumn of 1953, a German children's choir from the small town of Obernkirchen travelled to the equally-small north Wales town of Llangollen to take part in the annual International Eisteddfod - an arts and music festival - and stole the show with a merry little song celebrating the joys of roaming their native mountains laden with lederhosen and rucksacks.

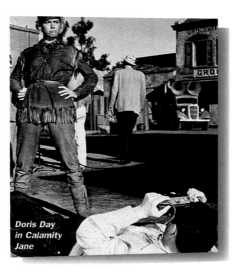

Doris Day in Calamity Jane

Picked up by radio presenters who knew a good marching song when they heard it, the German-language original of the song became an instant airtime hit, and The Obernkirchen Children's Choir was persuaded to trill an English version by Parlophone Records.

Shooting into the British charts at number 12 in January, *The Happy Wanderer* would spend a staggering five months in the Top 20, only being held off the top spot in April by English vocal group The Stargazers' I See The Moon. Ironically, The Stargazers had also recorded *The Happy Wanderer,* but their version had been stomped into oblivion by the Obernkirchen crew.

In America, keen ears at London Records spotted the hiking anthem's potential, and a version by Frank Weir was rushed out to give Weir an eventual number 4 hit, his main opposition being from Henri Rene who reached a 14 peak in July before wandering off into the sunset.

HALEY HIT HERALDS NEW MUSIC

Although it would be almost two years before the term became widely used, rock 'n' roll gained its first major international exposure this year when Bill Haley & The Comets scored a trans-Atlantic hit with *Shake, Rattle & Roll.* Written by, and a huge R&B hit for Joe Turner, the song was only one of a number of songs by black artists being picked up, cleaned up and recorded successfully by white acts - The Crew Cuts' hit *Sh-Boom* being a notable case in point.

An American number 1 and a UK Top 20 entrant in October, the Canadian-born, Cleveland-based Crew Cuts' record was so homogenized it could just as easily have been written by some Tin Pan Alley hack and not by The Chords, the black doo-wop team who'd scored with it in the R&B charts earlier in the year.

Haley's *Shake, Rattle & Roll,* on the other hand, at least retained some of the verve and attack of the original. It

was a sound which rang teenage bells, put it into the US charts in September (where it stayed until February 1955), and gave the former country and western singer a UK Top 10 hit in January 1955.

TWO EDDIES FIGHT OVER PAPA

You couldn't imagine two more different rivals for a hit than Eddie Fisher and Eddie Calvert, but the American crooner and the English trumpet player found themselves locked in dispute early this year with wildly different versions of a Swiss melody.

In America, Philadelphia-born singer Eddie Fisher - a solid hit-maker since 1950 after being discovered by yet another Eddie, Cantor by name, who invited him to join his touring show after hearing Fisher sing in a Catskills resort hotel - had a number 1 million-seller with an English lyric version called *Oh! My Pa-Pa.*

In Britain, Eddie Calvert - a newly-arrived sensation billed as 'The Man With The Golden Trumpet' because his instrument was - began a 21-week run in the charts, eight of them at the top, with his debut single *Oh Mein Papa.*

As usual, both versions were released in the other's country, and it was Calvert who won the runner-up contest. He managed to inch *Oh Mein Papa* as high as number 9 in the US and sell a million copies. The best Eddie Fisher could manage in Britain was a brief number 18.

Eddie Calvert would go on to have a US smash with *Cherry Pink And Apple Blossom White* in 1955. Eddie Fisher? Oh, he'd marry Debbie Reynolds and Elizabeth Taylor and continue enjoying major chart success until 1967.

You figure who really won.

Eddie Calvert

1000 Killed In Algerian Earthquake

IT ONLY LASTED 12 SECONDS, but the earthquake which hit the Algerian town of Orleansville today left 1,000 people dead and overwhelming damage which local authorities believe make it likely that most of the town will have to be abandoned forever.

The Orleansville tremor was the most serious of the 70 which shook the north African country in less than 24 hours. Sixteen of the shocks were described as serious, leaving more than 36,000 homeless.

With a large number of apartment blocks, houses and large public buildings weakened by earlier shocks, the final large Orleansville tremor caused their collapse into streets already split by wide cracks and fissures.

As troops and relief workers moved in to begin digging dead and injured from the ruins, relief agencies said the death toll would have been even higher if many people had not already fled their homes after the early tremors. However, many had elected to remain with their possessions in the belief that the worst was over.

London Gets Comprehensive

A quiet revolution in London today when the capital's first comprehensive school opened its gates for pupils between the ages of 11 and 17.

Kidbrooke School was the first salvo in the Labour Party's bid to end a selective education system which tested children at the age of 11, awarded grammar school places to those who did well and consigned the rest to a secondary education many perceived as second-rate.

The west London school is to be the flagship of Labour's abolition of the 11+ exam system, with all children transferring to comprehensive schools with enlarged and improved facilities to deal with both the academically gifted and the less able.

Marciano Reign Continues

The remarkable career of world heavyweight champ Rocky Marciano was extended to 47 consecutive wins in New York tonight - and he put paid to the challenge of the only man ever to take him the distance.

Champion since 1952, when he took it from 'Jersey' Joe Walcott, the Massachusetts-born Marciano faced Ezzard Charles, the gifted fighter who'd become the bad guy of American boxing by beating an over-the-hill Joe Louis in 1950 and had forced Marciano to his sole points victory in June.

Although the 33 year old Charles launched a spirited early attack and hurt the champion's face badly, Marciano put one of his notorious bombs together in the eighth round to knock him out.

ARRIVALS

Born this month:
1: Leonard Slatkin, US conductor
8: Anne Diamond, British TV presenter, Cot Death Syndrome publicist
11: Richard Linley, British champion jockey
24: Marco Tardelli, Italian soccer star

DEPARTURES

Died this month:
8: André Derain, French painter

NEWS IN BRIEF

5: In Ireland, 28 passengers and crew aboard a Dutch KLM airliner died when it crashed into the River Shannon

19: Members of the Federation of Sun Clubs, a British nudist organization, held their first annual conference

24: Building workers uncovered the remains of a Roman temple dedicated to the god Mithras near The Mansion House, official residence of The Lord Mayor of London

27: In Japan, 1,700 reported drowned after a ferry capsized

28: The British Motor Company unveiled its new family saloon, the Austin Cambridge

Labour OKs German Re-Armament

It's almost 10 years since the end of World War II in Europe, but there are many in the former Allied countries still wary of plans to allow a rebuilt West Germany to form a new army.

Britain's opposition Labour Party has its fair share of opponents to German rearmament, but they were narrowly defeated at the party's annual conference today. After a heated debate, delegates for the leadership's motion to approve the creation of a revised Wermacht outnumbered those against.

'Seven Brides' Gives MGM A Super Smash

Big movie hit worldwide this autumn was the new MGM musical Seven Brides For Seven Brothers, an all-singing, all-dancing romp starring Howard Keel and Jane Powell. Directed by Stanley Donen, with songs by Johnny Mercer and Gene de Paul, it re-told the story of the rape of the Sabine women in Roman times, setting it in pioneer America and giving choreographer Michael Kidd the chance to create some stunning dance sequences for the healthy young men and women keen to do what comes naturally.

National Trust Buys Scottish Isle

Conservation may have become a fashionable interest in recent years, but the world's environmentalists have long been doing their best to ensure some of the best bits get saved for future generations. The National Trust for Scotland purchased the barely-populated Fair Isle, part of the Shetland island group off the north-west Scottish coast. A key resting place for numerous endangered migrant birds, Fair Isle also boasts a unique knitting style believed to have been introduced to ancestors of the 70 or so inhabitants in the 17th Century by survivors of the Spanish Armada.

Two US Officers Killed In Red Chinese Bomb Raid

STOPPING JUST SHORT OF actually launching an invasion of the Nationalist stronghold of Formosa - a move President Eisenhower had warned him against last month - Communist Chinese leader Mao Tse-Tung today ordered a massive bombardment of Quemoy, another Chiang Kai-Shek island just off the mainland

During the five-hour shelling, two US Army officers were among those killed. Their deaths are sure to rebound on the communists and lead to increased American support for the Formosan regime, for which Quemoy - scene of their first major victory over the communists in 1949 - remains a strategic possession.

Within 24 hours, and while the attack on Quemoy was resumed, Nationalist forces launched a major attack on the communist-held Tateng Island.

Mao's muscle flexing may have been a last-minute show to reinforce his domestic position, confirmed by his re-election as party chairman by The People's Congress on September 27. His new deputy is General Chu-Teh.

Going Up In The World

Powered flight has been a reality for half a century, but until today the only direction planes could go was forwards. To be precise, forwards and up, then more forwards until they slowed and came to earth, still going forwards.

All that changed with the aircraft revealed in Britain by Rolls-Royce. Nicknamed 'The Flying Bedstead' it can, like a helicopter, rise vertically into the air. Then it goes forwards.

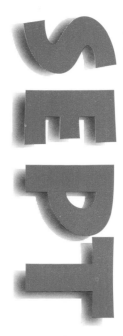

Marilyn And DiMaggio Split

The nine-month marriage of baseball legend Joe DiMaggio and Hollywood screen siren Marilyn Monroe ended officially today when the actress filed for divorce.

Although Monroe's divorce petition cited conflicting career demands as grounds for annulment, reliable gossip says the two had proved to be ill-matched from the start.

DiMaggio's inability to handle his wife's apparent willingness to display too much of her natural charms to the cameras - especially the legendary air-vent sequence in the forthcoming Seven Year Itch (pictured) - had led to screaming rows and physical abuse. Monroe's inability to remain a one-man woman and have at least one extra-marital dalliance probably didn't help keep them together.

Ho Chi Minh Returns To Hanoi

North Vietnam's communist leader Ho Chi Minh returned to Hanoi today, ending an eight year period of exile during which he had masterminded the Viet Minh's operations against French forces.

Ho's return was a deliberately low-key affair. The man his followers call 'Uncle Ho' had asked residents to go back to work, although the capital did pay tribute to the thousands of Viet Minh - led by commander General Vo Nguyen Giap - marched through sectors the French had evacuated the previous day under the terms of the armistice.

US ships had moved into the area on October 8 to begin transporting thousands of refugees heading for South Vietnam.

Metal Fatigue Blamed For Comet Crashes

A SMALL PART OF THE CABIN roof containing the radio direction-finding aerial was today identified as the crucial weak-spot in BOAC's Comet jet airliners, three of which have mysteriously crashed in the past year - one in India and two in the Mediterranean.

Since the last crash in April, off the Italian island of Stromboli with a loss of all 21 passengers and seven crew, experts at The Royal Aircraft Establishment in Farnborough have been carrying out exhaustive tests to locate the Comet's fatal flaw.

Suspicions that metal fatigue was to blame appear to have been confirmed with the discovery that the cabin roof section is 'quite likely' to break up under the stress of take-off. The scientific results have been passed to the official inquiry investigating the Comet disasters.

Golding's Masterpiece Published

Literary critics were unanimous in their praise of Lord Of The Flies, a futuristic novel by William Golding first published in London today. The book, which Golding wrote in spare time from his duties as a teacher of English in a Salisbury grammar school, describes the descent into barbarism of a group of schoolboys stranded on a tropical isle after a plane crash. Described as a brilliant analogy of post-nuclear society, it would become an international best-seller, be filmed twice and help Golding win the 1983 Nobel Prize for Literature.

Havoc As Hazel Hits America

One hundred and eighteen people were reported killed today in the US as Hurricane Hazel, one of the biggest in recent memory, tore across eight eastern seaboard states to create a swathe of destruction.

Storm-driven tides wreaked millions of dollars worth of damage along the coast, while towns hundreds of miles inland were smashed by 100 mph winds and floods.

President Eisenhower declared the areas worst affected disaster zones, so enabling local authorities to draw on Federal aid for their repair and rebuilding programmes.

OCTOBER 26

Nasser Escapes Assassination Attempt

EGYPTIAN PRIME MINISTER Colonel Gamal Nasser missed death by inches tonight when a gunman opened fire during a rally to celebrate the planned withdrawal of British troops from the Suez Canal Zone. One of the shots hit a light bulb above Nasser's head.

The attempted assassination happened in the port of Alexandria, where thousands had gathered to hear Nasser spell out his plans now the Anglo-Egyptian agreement has been signed to ensure all British troops will quit Egypt within 20 months.

The Prime Minister maintained his composure as bullets flew from the crowd. 'Catch that man', he shouted. 'Gamal Abdel Nasser is safe. My blood is for you!'

The would-be assassin was captured and later named by police as 20 year old Mahmoud Abdel Latif, a Cairo tinsmith and member of the extremist Moslem Brotherhood. Within hours, hundreds of Moslem Brotherhood supporters had been rounded up in Alexandria and Cairo. The next day, a mob attacked and burned the organization's Cairo HQ while police concentrated on hunting down Brotherhood leaders.

The attack would only serve to strengthen Nasser's hand as he fought to gain absolute power. Having subdued cautious moderates among the Revolutionary Command Council and defeated the old politicians, he now had an excuse to come down hard on the Moslem Brotherhood.

OCTOBER 29

Dock Strike Hits British Sea Trade

A month-long strike by more than 50,000 British dock workers was ended today after union leaders met with Sir Walter Monckton, the Minister of Labour. It is estimated that the country's sea trade was cut by half during the strike, called in protest at new work conditions.

The strike began in London and, at its peak, involved two-thirds of the total work-force. They claimed that changes to the national Dock Labour Scheme would impose a regime of compulsory overtime - something the government denied.

OCTOBER 2

NATO Admits West Germany

The international rehabilitation of West Germany took a giant leap forward today when a nine-power conference in London voted to admit the wartime enemy into NATO, the strategic defence alliance formed to protect Europe and the US from attack by Soviet and east European forces. Although West Germany's membership of NATO is recognition of its conversion from enemy to ally, especially as it borders so much with front-line communist countries, it is not to be allowed to own its own nuclear weapons. These will continue to be positioned in US, British and French military bases in West Germany.

Chataway Smashes 5,000m Record

London witnessed one of the greatest races in modern athletics history today when the 23 year old Oxford University and British international Chris Chataway slashed five seconds off the world 5,000 metre record.

The race, highlight of a London v Moscow meeting held at the White City stadium, saw Chataway defeat European champion Vladimir Kuts with a superb display of strategic running.

Watched by a cheering crowd and a live TV audience, Chataway tracked Kuts throughout the race, kicked himself clear in the final straight and crossed the line in a record 13 mins 15.6 seconds.

OCTOBER 5
BOB GELDOF

It says something about our times that the single biggest and most successful international response to a tragedy was initiated and eventually masterminded by a rock musician too determined (some say arrogant) to take 'no' as an answer to his outrageous demands.

Dublin-born Bob Geldof's reaction to BBC television coverage of the 1984 Ethiopian famine was to call Ultravox singer Midge Ure and write *Do They Know It's Christmas?* as a fund-raising song. Aware that sales were likely to be minimal if it was recorded by his over-the-hill band The Boomtown Rats, Geldof pressured a Who's Who of British rock to participate under the name Band Aid, got free studio time and talked every major record company to press and distribute it for nothing.

The single was rush-released, became the UK's immediate number 1 and also sold more than 1.5 million in the US to help raise £8 million ($16m).

American star Harry Belafonte picked up on Geldof's enthusiasm and recruited a host of US stars to do likewise under the name USA For Africa. Their single, *We Are The World,* went to number 1 in just about every country with electricity. Geldof, meanwhile, had visited Ethiopia for himself and decided to harness the international music community's goodwill with a huge

Sir Bob

event in July 1985.

Staged simultaneously at London's Wembley Stadium and the JFK Stadium in Philadelphia and broadcast live all round the world, Live Aid combined the talents of scores of superstars only too willing to give their time to raise many millions more. Bob Geldof, later given an honorary knighthood by the Queen, had achieved his stated dream of changing the world into a global jukebox. Not bad for a 31 year old Irish punk rocker with a severe attitude problem.

MARCH 3
NOEL GAY

One of Britain's most successful songwriters in the 1930s and 40s, Noel Gay (born Richard Moxon Armitage) remains best known for his stage musical *Me And My Girl*.

London's longest-running show in the 30s, his story of the cockney who inherits a title became a huge surprise smash on Broadway in the 1980s when revived with actor Robert Lindsey in the lead role. Lindsey then returned to London to launch a British revival which packed audiences in until 1993.

A shrewd businessman, Gay also built a formidably-successful music publishing company which handled *Me And My Girl* and the many standards he wrote, including *Run Rabbit Run* (a WWII hit for Bud Flanagan), *I Took My Harp To A Party* (Gracie Fields), *Leaning On A Lamp-Post* (George Formby) and the much-recorded *The Sun Has Got His Hat On*.

JULY 18
RICKY SKAGGS

Ricky Skaggs' raising in the Kentucky mountains was full of traditional music and strict religion, both of which continue to play dominant roles in his life. A multi-skilled instrumentalist (mandolin, fiddle, guitar and banjo), he appeared on TV with the legendary bluegrass team of Flatt and Scruggs when only seven years old and became a full-time member of the Ralph Stanley band when he was just fifteen.

After a successful period leading his own bands, in 1977 Skaggs joined Emmylou Harris' Hot Band to bring his considerable talents to the attention of a broad international country-rock audience. In 1980 he began a new solo career which has produced 10 number 1 singles and resulted in him being voted the Country Music Association's Male Vocalist of the Year in 1982, Entertainer of the Year in 1985 and, with his wife Sharon White, being named Duo of the Year in 1987.

That same year saw Skaggs win a Grammy Award for Best Country Instrumental with *Wheel Hoss*, a number which - along with *Country Boy* - has emerged as a Ricky Skaggs trademark as he continues to tour the world.

Johnson To Head Senate In Democrat Congress

LYNDON BAINES JOHNSON, the 46 year old Texan senator, is to become the new head of the US Senate in a Congress now under Democratic Party control since a string of victories in America's mid-term elections wrested superiority from President Eisenhower's Republicans.

The tall, rangy Johnson is a noted in-fighter and manipulator. Capable of great generosity, he is also happy to use dirty tricks against political and business opponents, as his rapid rise through the notoriously-murky waters of Texas state politics proves.

A self-made millionaire with extensive oil and communications interests - he owns a number of successful radio stations - Johnson is being widely tipped as a man to watch.

His carefully-cultivated folksy image belies an incisive intelligent politician whose influence can only grow as the Democrats begin to erode President Eisenhower's dominance of national policy-making and they introduce their own domestic measures.

Modern Master Matisse Paints His Last

Henri Matisse, one of the greatest and most influential painters of the 20th century, died today at his home in the South of France. Disabled by arthritis since 1948, he had spent the last few years creating simple, brilliantly-coloured pictures from cut-up paper. He was 85 years old.

Trained as a lawyer, Matisse began painting

Dimbleby Rejects ITV Offer

With commercial television due to be launched in Britain next year, owners of the first Independent Television (ITV) franchise licenses are busy trying to poach the BBC's best-known and most polished performers, and they're offering big money. One BBC stalwart who will not be making the move is Richard Dimbleby, the man chosen to commentate live when the coronation of Queen Elizabeth was televised last year, and the first face to appear on-screen in 1950 when the BBC beamed live pictures from France in an inaugural link-up with Europe.

France Sends Troops To Riot-Torn Algeria

With nationalist-inspired riots leaving a trail of destruction and death through its north African colony of Algeria, France today announced it is to send a large number of troop reinforcements to help stabilize the situation.

The government decision was given by Minister of the Interior François Mitterand, and came after 10 days of disturbances believed to be the work of independence-seeking terrorists led by the exiled Ahmed Ben Bella, who is now based in Cairo. On November 1, seven people were reported dead and 14 wounded when farmsteads, military and police establishments were targeted in the area around Aures.

US Institute Confirms Smoking-Cancer Link

Following widespread tobacco industry criticism of the June report claiming a link between smoking and cancer in the over 50s, US health authorities were presented with more ammunition today.

In a comprehensive and detailed report designed to forestall any response by pro-tobacco apologists, the US National Cancer Institute claimed its research proves a definite link between cigarette smoking, cancer and other bronchial complaints.

full-time in 1890, initially influenced by the likes of Neo-Impressionists such as Gauguin and Vincent van Gogh, but his own distinctive use of form and colour was described as 'fauvre', or 'wild beast' - the name subsequently attached to the movement which followed his lead.

A sculptor, theatre and book designer, muralist and creator of the acclaimed decorative scheme for the Chapelle de Rosaire in Venice, his later naturalistic works inspired innumerable younger artists.

Controversy As Churchill Portrait Unveiled

IT'S COMMON ENOUGH FOR a grateful nation to commission one of its leading artists to paint a portrait of someone who has achieved international pre-eminence or given their country special service. So the decision of British MPs to honour Sir Winston Churchill with a major painting, which would be unveiled on his 80th birthday, was universally applauded.

The choice of artist Graham Sutherland had raised eyebrows, however. Very much a modern painter, his unflattering warts-and-all portraits of beautician Helena Rubinstein and playwright Somerset Maugham should have warned the commissioning committee they weren't going to have a rose-tinted portrayal of the old warrior.

So it proved today, when Sutherland's painting was produced at a televised ceremony held at Westminster Hall. An uncompromising depiction of an unsmiling, almost arrogant Churchill, it drew gasps of dismay from the assembled worthies and an uncharacteristic display of diplomacy from its subject. Confining his distaste to describing Sutherland's work as 'a remarkable example of modern art', he raised laughter by adding: 'It certainly combines force and candour'.

Behind the scenes, Lady Clementine Churchill was vitriolic. While it was rumoured she'd physically attacked the painting, it appears she ordered it to be stored away. It would never be hung, as planned, on permanent display in the House of Commons.

'Spy' Hiss Released From Prison

Alger Hiss, the former US State Department employee jailed in 1950 after two controversial trials on espionage charges, was released from prison today after serving 44 months for perjury.

An early victim of Senator Joe McCarthy's anti-communist witch-hunt, Hiss was first accused of being a Russian agent in 1948 after a hearing of the House Un-American Activities Committee.

His first trial ended with a hung jury, and while no evidence of espionage was presented at his second trial in January 1950, Hiss was given a harsh five-year sentence for perjury after admitting having once owned a typewriter used to copy confidential and secret government documents.

Nasser Takes Full Control

With all important Moslem Brotherhood figures in captivity awaiting trial for treason and conspiracy and the old political guard comfortably compliant, the only real obstacle to Nasser's complete control of the country was the continued presence of President Neguib. That ended on November 13 when the Prime Minister overthrew Neguib in a lightning coup and placed him under house arrest. Four days later Nasser assumed all Neguib's powers, and while this effectively made him Egyptian President and Prime Minister, he did not adopt the first title.

NOV

Congress Condemns Witch-Hunter McCarthy

IT LOOKS LIKE THE END of the road for Joe McCarthy (pictured), the Wisconsin Senator whose increasingly arrogant chairmanship of the House Un-American Activities Committee in the past year has outraged and alarmed even once-loyal Republican party supporters of his anti-communist investigations.

Today the US Senate voted 67-22 to censure McCarthy for 'conduct unbecoming a Senator'. The once-inviolable witch-hunter's fall from grace is best illustrated by the fact that half of the Republicans voted against him.

During the near six years of his chairmanship, McCarthy treated the Committee as a personal fiefdom, stoking the coals of understandable cold war suspicion of communism into a red-hot fire of paranoia. While his activities undeniably led to a number of covert communists being uncovered, many innocent and naive liberals were ruined by his hectoring interrogations and willingness to accept unsupported hearsay evidence.

Architect of his own demise when his treatment of senior military figures appalled ordinary Americans and President Eisenhower - a former general, remember - McCarthy's increasingly wild allegations of communist infiltration of the CIA accelerated his fall.

Although McCarthy said he intended to continue investigations into alleged defence establishment infiltration, he will have to give way to a new Democrat chairman in January. Broken by the censure vote, McCarthy would slip into the shadows and die within three years.

Italian Xmas For Whitfield

Surprisingly, there was no big Christmas hit in the United States this year - not even a reappearance of stalwart standards like *White Christmas* or *Rudolph The Red-Nosed Reindeer*. And the only holiday hit in Britain was sung in Italian!

The song was *Santo Natale (Holy Christmas)*, by one of Britain's biggest heart-throbs of the early fifties, David Whitfield. Whitfield had a thing about Italian songs. His biggest-ever hit was the near-operatic *Cara Mia*, sales of which would help put him alongside the likes of Elvis Presley, Pat Boone, Perry Como and Frank Sinatra when a breakdown of the UK's most successful singles acts between 1954 and 1959 was compiled.

For the record, America's top single in this month was *Mr Sandman*, by The Chordettes.

DECEMBER 17

Birth Of New Giant

Destined to become an international giant in the petrochemical field, the infant British Petroleum was born in London today, thanks largely to the activities of Islamic fundamentalists in Iran!

BP's creation came to ensure that the British oil industry continued to maintain an interest - initially 40 per cent - in the recently-nationalized National Iranian Oil Company.

While Iran had vast reserves of 'black gold', it still needed the technical expertise and marketing skills of a Western partner. As British oil companies had developed Iranian oil resources since 1909 and successive British governments had actively supported the Shah's regime, the formation of BP made complete sense.

DECEMBER 18

Air Crashes In US And UK

Not a good month for two major airlines attempting to persuade more people to switch their travel plans and take to the skies. With headlines about BOAC's Comet disasters still fresh, safety plays as big a role in carriers' sales-pitches as speed and comfort.

But on December 18, US and Italian broadcasts were filled with news of fresh disaster when an Italian Airways passenger flight crashed while attempting to land at New Jersey's Idlewild Airport, with 26 deaths.

BOAC's year ended even more tragically when, on December 25, one of their Stratocruiser fleet crashed at Prestwick Airport, in Scotland. Although fire and rescue crews managed to save eight of those on board, 28 passengers and crew were killed.

ARRIVALS
Born this month:
11: Jermaine Jackson, US pop singer, member of Jackson family
13: Jim Davidson, UK comedian, TV host
21: Chris Evert Lloyd, US tennis champion
25: Steve Wariner, US country music singer

DEPARTURES
Died this month:
20: James Hilton, UK novelist, screenwriter (*Goodbye Mr. Chips, Lost Horizon*)

DECEMBER 18

Evita's Spirit Wins Divorce Rights

Although she died of cancer back in July 1952, the spirit of Eva Peron - known to her millions of Argentinian followers as 'Evita' - lives on. It is acknowledged that her influence also lives on and played a huge part in today's decision to legalize divorce in Argentina.

Vilified by her many opponents as corrupt and accused of being personally involved in the torture and disappearance of enemies, Evita was adored by Argentina's poor. A champion of female rights, she succeeded in winning women the vote, and had begun to fight male chauvinism and the Roman Catholic Church to make divorce legal before she died. Evita's name and memory were invoked by her husband, President Juan Peron, as he steered the divorce bill through to victory.

DECEMBER 18

Rioters Stone British Bars In Cyprus

INCREASING GREEK CYPRIOT CALLS for independence from Britain and union with Greece reached danger-point today in Limassol when British troops were ordered to fire on a gang of youths who'd torn down a Union Jack flying over a police station and raised the Greek flag in its place. Two of the rioters were injured.

In other sections of the south coast resort, mobs of Cypriots hurled stones at British-owned bars, overturned and set a van alight. More than 40 were arrested by police, who had to handle more trouble when a small group of Turks began smashing the windows of Greek shops.

The riots were sparked off by a United Nations decision to shelve a Greek government demand that Cyprus be given the right of self-determination. With both Greece and Turkey claiming rights to an island already split between two incompatible ethnic groups sharing only a desire for independence, Cyprus is set to provide Britain with yet one more hot-bed of resistance to its colonial legacy.

DECEMBER 10

Literature Nobel For Hemingway

American novelist, big-game hunter and bullfighting buff Ernest Hemingway was awarded the coveted Nobel Prize for Literature in the Swedish capital, Stockholm, today.

A stretcher-bearer during WWI, a combatant and war correspondent during the Spanish Civil War in the 1930s and a reporter in WWII, Hemingway drew on those experiences for his best-selling novels *A Farewell To Arms, Death In The Afternoon, For Whom The Bell Tolls* and *The Sun Also Rises*.

He began writing while living in Paris in the early 20s. That story also helped win the Illinois-born Hemingway a 1953 Pulitzer Prize for Literature. In failing health, Hemingway would shoot himself in 1961 when his health began to fail.

Suspects rounded up
during Cyprus riots

UN Awarded Peace Prize

DECEMBER 10

A rare moment in the history of the Nobel Prize awards today in the Norwegian capital, Oslo. The annual Peace Prize, usually presented to an individual or individuals the award committee consider has made an exemplary contribution to establishing or furthering international peace, was awarded to an organization.

For once, the choice of recipient - The Office of the United Nations High Commissioner for Refugees - was applauded almost unanimously.

Since its creation in 1945, the UN's Refugee Commission had organized and supervised the safe movement of millions fleeing the many wars, big and small, which continued to beset the world. True to its charter, it tries to care for all, regardless of race, creed or political belief.

YOUR 1954 HOROSCOPE

Unlike most Western horoscope systems which group astrological signs into month-long periods based on the influence of 12 constellations, the Chinese believe that those born in the same year of their calendar share common qualities, traits and weaknesses with one of 12 animals - Rat, Ox, Tiger, Rabbit, Dragon, Snake, Horse, Sheep, Monkey, Rooster, Dog or Pig.

They also allocate the general attributes of five natural elements - Earth, Fire, Metal, Water, Wood - and an overall positive or negative aspect to each sign to summarize its qualities.

If you were born between February 14, 1953 and February 2, 1954, you are a Snake. As this book is devoted to the events of 1954, let's take a look at the sign which governs those born between February 3 that year and February 16, 1955 - The Year of The Horse.

THE HORSE
(FEBRUARY 3, 1954-FEBRUARY 16, 1955)
ELEMENT: WOOD ASPECT: +

Horses are born with vast inbuilt energy resources, are very strong and active, and prefer to be busy all the time. They are at their best when their stamina and physical resources are put to the test, are both quick to catch on and efficient in their undertakings.

Horses are pleasant, lively people with the ability to put people at ease instantly. Gifted with good humour and *bonhomie*, they bring good cheer to those around them.

Horses are characterized by a strong need for freedom and independence, and don't like to be tied down by commitments. As soon as someone makes too many demands or restricts their freedom, Horses will kick out, rebel and run away towards new horizons.

As they tend to act on impulse to remain their own master or mistress, there is a strong sense of unpredictability about Horses. It makes them appear very casual in their attitude to life. However, as much as they don't want their lives to be ruled by anyone but themselves, Horses are very tolerant and unresentful towards those who don't fulfil their commitments.

Despite their carefree outlook on life, Horses can be very loyal to family and friends and are not afraid of taking on necessary responsibilities. They have incisive and quick-witted minds and make accurate judgements. Being very practical and logical, they are able to deal with several projects at the same time.

Horses have a strong sense of what they should look like and are attracted to refinement and elegance in their choice of appearance. Very diplomatic, they possess extraordinary charm and fall in love easily. They find it hard to keep their own counsel - whatever they feel or think must be expressed on the spot. They find it impossible to keep secrets as gossiping and chatting are two of their favourite hobbies.

Horses are easy-going, tolerant, affable people who have the need to feel free, be able to move forward, and to accept and deal with their responsibilities.

FAMOUS HORSES

HRH Princess Margaret	**Zola Budd**
HRH Prince Michael of Kent	South African athlete
Neil Armstrong	**Neil Kinnock**
astronaut	Socialist politician, ex leader of the Labour party
Clint Eastwood	
actor, producer/director	**Paul McCartney**
Billy Graham	rock singer, writer, producer
Christian evangelist	**Barbara Streisand**
Bob Geldof	singer, actress, producer/director
rock star, philanthropist (Live Aid)	**Chris Evert**
	tennis champion